Lecture Notes in Control and Information Sciences

Edited by M. Thoma and A. Wyner

24 40

W9-DFR-318

94

Hari Krishna

Computational Complexity of Bilinear Forms

Algebraic Coding Theory and Applications to Digital Communication Systems

Springer-Verlag
Berlin Heidelberg New York
London Paris Tokyo

Author

Hari Krishna
Department of Electrical and Computer Engineering
Link Hall
Syracuse University
Syracuse, NY 13244-1240
USA

QA
268
.K75
1987
1

ISBN 3-540-17661-6 Springer-Verlag Berlin Heidelberg New York
ISBN 0-387-17661-6 Springer-Verlag New York Berlin Heidelberg

Library of Congress Cataloging in Publication Data
Krishna, Hari
Computational complexity of bilinear forms.
(Lecture notes in control and information sciences ; 94)
1. Coding theory.
2. Computational complexity.
3. Forms, Bilinear.
I. Title.
II. Series.
QA268.K75 1987 005.1 87-4889
ISBN 0-387-17661-6 (U.S.)

© Springer-Verlag Berlin, Heidelberg 1987
Printed in Germany

Offsetprinting: Mercedes-Druck, Berlin
Binding: B. Helm, Berlin
2161/3020-543210

To
My Parents

PREFACE

In this work, the correspondence between linear (n,k,d) codes and algorithms for computing a system of k bilinear forms over $GF(p^m)$ is explored. A number of properties are established for the linear codes that follow from a computational procedure of this type. A particular system of bilinear forms is considered and a class of linear codes is derived with varying k and d parameters. The codelength n is equal to the multiplicative complexity of the computation of an aperiodic convolution and an efficient computation thereof leads to the shortest codes possible using this approach. Many of the codes obtained are optimal or near optimal in terms of their rate and distance. A new decoding procedure for this class of codes is presented which exploits the block structure of the generator matrix. This decoding procedure can be realised using parallel architecture. These codes are characterized by their modular structure which, in turn, can be used to design codes with variable minimum distance but having a similar encoding/decoding procedure. Several observations which are very important from a practical standpoint are made on the nature of the codes obtained as a result of the computational method used for the system of bilinear forms. Such a computation can be generalized to include other bilinear forms and the related classes of codes. The concept of generalized hybrid automatic repeat request (GH-ARQ) for adaptive error-control in digital communication systems is discussed.

This scheme utilises the redundant information available upon successive retransmissions in an efficient manner so as to provide high throughput during poor channel conditions. The class of linear codes derived in this work, is proposed as an excellent candidate for such an application. One unique feature of this class of codes is that the encoder/decoder configuration does not change as the length of the code is varied. As a result, the receiver uses the same decoder for decoding the received information after every retransmission while the error-correcting capability of the code increases, thereby leading to an improved performance and minimum complexity for the overall system implementation.

Hari Krishna, Ph.D.
Concordia University, 1985

ACKNOWLEDGEMENTS

I take this opportunity to express my gratitude towards Dr. Salvatore D. Morgera for his immaculate supervision of this research work. He has been friend, philosopher, and guide to me. Thanks Sal.

I would like to thank Mrs. Madeleine Klein for her excellent typing of a difficult manuscript. Thanks are also due to Ms. Anita Claassen for her patient typing of the research papers that formed the basis of this thesis.

I also acknowledge all the help and moral support extended to me by Dr. R.V. Patel and Dr. V. Ramachandran from time to time.

Last, but not least, I thank, Anita, Lina, Madeleine, Monica, and my other friends for sharing my good as well as bad times with equal vigour.

This research work was supported by Canada NSERC Grant A0912 and Québec FCAC Grant EQ-350.

TABLE OF CONTENTS

LIST OF ABBREVIATIONS AND IMPORTANT SYMBOLS

(n,k,d) : A code V of length n, dimension k, and minimum distance d

$GF(p^m)$, $GF(q)$: Galois field of p^m or q elements

ARQ : Automatic repeat request

GH-ARQ : Generalised hybrid-ARQ

CRT : Chinese remainder theorem

KM : Krishna-Morgera

BCH : Bose-Chaudhary-Hocquenghem

RS : Reed-Solomon

ψ : A system of bilinear forms

F : An arbitrary field

a_i : An element of F (constant)

$x_1, x_2, \ldots$: Indeterminates

$y_1, y_2, \ldots$: Indeterminates

$z_1, z_2, \ldots$: Indeterminates

Superscript T : Matrix (or vector) transposition

$\underline{x}, \underline{y}, \underline{z}, \underline{u}, \underline{v}, \underline{a}, \underline{b}, \underline{c}$: Vectors of appropriate dimensions

X, A, B, C : Matrices of appropriate dimensions

C : Generator matrix of a (n,k,d) code

$\rho(x)$: Row rank of X over F

Φ : Dual system of bilinear forms

$\phi_0, \phi_1, \ldots$: Dual bilinear forms

N : Length of aperiodic convolution

$Z(u)$	:	Generating polynomial of the sequence $z_0, z_1, \ldots, z_{k-1}$
$Y(u)$	:	Generating polynomial of the sequence $y_0, y_1, \ldots, y_{d-1}$
$\Phi(u)$	:	Generating polynomial of the sequence $\phi_0, \phi_1, \ldots, \phi_{N-1}$
$P(u)$	:	A polynomial
$P_i(u)$	:	ith polynomial factor of $P(u)$
$\deg[P(u)]$	:	Degree of the polynomial $P(u)$
$Z_i(u)$	:	$Z(u)$ reduced modulo $P_i(u)$
$Y_i(u)$	:	$Y(u)$ reduced modulo $P_i(u)$
$\Phi_i(u)$	:	$\Phi(u)$ reduced modulo $P_i(u)$
$\equiv$	:	Equivalent to
$M(\alpha_i)$	:	Multiplicative complexity of the computation $\Phi_i(u) \equiv Z_i(u)Y_i(u)$ modulo $P_i(u)$
s	:	Number of wraparound coefficients
$\bar{Z}(u)$	:	The polynomial $Z(u^{-1}) u^{k-1}$
$\bar{Y}(u)$	:	The polynomial $Y(u^{-1}) u^{d-1}$
α_i	:	$\deg[P_i(u)]$
$Z(u,u_1)$	:	Polynomial $Z(u)$ expressed as two-dimensional polynomial
$Y(u,u_1)$	:	Polynomial $Y(u)$ expressed as two-dimensional polynomial
$\Phi(u,u_1)$	:	Polynomial $\Phi(u)$ expressed as two-dimensional polynomial
m_i	:	ith multiplication
$\ell.i.$	:	Linearly independent
C_i	:	ith block of the generator matrix C
n_i	:	Length of the block C_i (Also, $n_i = M(\alpha_i)$)

$\|x\|$	:	Absolute value of x
$\underline{c}$	:	Codevector
$[x]$	:	Largest integer less than or equal to x
σ_i	:	Number of errors in part of a received vector corresponding to C_i
π	:	Set of integers
π_i	:	ith subset of π
FEC	:	Forward error control
ACK	:	Acknowledgement
NACK	:	Nonacknowledgement
V_0	:	Code used for error-detection
V_1	:	Code used for error-correction
I	:	Block of length n
$\tilde{I}$	:	Received block corresponding to I
$P(I)$	:	Parity block for I based on V_1
$\tilde{P}(I)$	:	Received block corresponding to P(I)
$I(\tilde{P})$	:	Inverse of $\tilde{P}(I)$
$\hat{I}$	:	Decoded block corresponding to I, based on V_1
G	:	Generator matrix of V_1
G_i	:	ith subblock of G
$V_1^{(i)}$	:	ith subcode of V_1
ε	:	Channel bit error rate
$Int[x]$	:	Integral part of x
A	:	Numbers of transmissions required to recover I successfully
$E[A]$	:	Expected value of A
$Pr(.)$	:	Probability of the event
η	:	Throughput efficiency of the ARQ scheme

S_j :   jth GH-ARQ scheme

$P_{S_j}[i]$:   Probability of the event that for S_j, the receiver recovers I successfully in i transmissions

P_{e_i} :   Probability of undetected error for the ith transmissions

P_e :   Max (P_{e_i}, i = 1,2,...)

P_c :   Probability of the event that the ith transmission of I is received error-free

E :   Event that a block containing undetectable errors is accepted in GH-ARQ scheme

P_f :   Min (P_{e_i}, i = 1,2,...)

LIST OF TABLES

CHAPTER 1

INTRODUCTION

The theories of digital signal processing and error-correcting codes have historically different origins. In spite of this, it is possible to adopt the philosophy that the theory of error-correcting codes may be considered as a branch of digital signal processing, since error-correction coding is essentially a signal processing technique used to improve the reliability of communication on digital channels. Error-correction coding has been developed by algebraists while electrical engineers have developed the techniques used in digital signal processing. Both subjects rely heavily on the properties, techniques and algorithms for aperiodic and periodic convolution and Fourier transformation. The relationship between time domain sequences and their Fourier transforms is used extensively in the analysis, design, and implementation of digital signal processing and error-correcting systems. The major difference in the two theories may be attributed to different number systems: digital signal processing techniques employ to a great extent the field of complex numbers (infinite number of elements) as compared to error-correcting codes which employ Galois fields (finite number of elements).

Any codeword corresponding to an arbitrary code may be treated as a sequence such that each element of the sequence belongs to $GF(q)$, where $GF(q)$ represents the Galois field of q elements. Fourier transforms defined in a Galois field play an important role in the design and analysis of coding schemes. For example, cyclic codes can be defined as codes in which each codeword is a sequence having certain prespecified spectral components equal to zero [1]. Thus, alternative techniques for encoding such codes can be realised by using frequency domain properties of the codes.

A number of fast and efficient algorithms which were developed for digital signal processing can also be used to reduce the complexity of the decoding procedures of coding schemes. Furthermore, fast algorithms may be used to obtain accelerated procedures for the decoding of several coding schemes, thereby resulting in more efficient and improved decoding procedures.

Fourier transforms defined over a finite field, and having the cyclic convolution property, were first described by Pollard [2]. The use of these transform techniques in coding schemes was discussed by Gore [3] and was extended further by Chien et al [4], and Lempel et al [5]. The relationship between the fast Fourier transform algorithms and the complexity of decoding was described by Justesen [6] and Sarwate [7].

In this work, we study the relationship between the multiplicative complexity associated with the computation of a class of algebraic functions called bilinear forms and linear error-correcting codes. Based on the computation of a particular bilinear form, a new class of linear error-correcting codes is derived from the bilinear algorithms used for aperiodic convolution of certain sequences. Such a class of codes possesses certain unique feautures in terms of the code parameters, code family relationships, and encoding and decoding procedures. Decoding procedures for small codes form the basis of the overall decoding procedure for the codes generated. Therefore, it is possible to design a decoder that processes parts of the received vector independently, thereby leading to a parallel architecture for the decoder implementation, a desirable feature in high data rate communication systems. Also, it is possible to vary the error-correcting capability of the codes very easily, and therefore, a number of different codes can be incorporated into a single encoder/decoder design. It is interesting to note that due to the parallel architecture of the decoder, the processing throughput of the decoder remains the same for all codes incorporated in one design.

The structure of the codes is such that they can be very effectively used to obtain adaptive error-correcting capability for digital communication over channels having non-stationary error rates. Based on the codes generated, an error control scheme is proposed and analysed which can be used to provide high throughput for digital communication systems that use the automatic repeat request technique. The proposed scheme takes into consideration all the properties of the codes so as to keep the complexity of the overall scheme to a minimum. Due to the unique properties of the codes derived in this work, it may be possible to use them to improve the performance of communication systems which require codes of a specialised nature. This forms the topic of ongoing research work.

Readers not familiar with the theory of error-correcting codes may find references [8], [9], and [10] useful. A comprehensive coverage of algebraic coding theory and of the relevant relationships between algebraic coding theory and digital signal processing is contained in reference [1]. Also, the reader is referred to [11] and [12] for the mathematical analysis and description of the theory of polynomial algebra as used in digital signal processing.

1.1 Major Contributions of the Work

This work unifies a number of concepts which are fundamental to the theories of error-correcting codes and digital signal processing. The major contributions of the work can be summarised as follows:

(1) Based on algorithms for aperiodic convolution of two sequences, a new class of error-correcting codes is described in Chapter 4.

(2) This class of codes possesses several interesting features which are highlighted in Sections 4.1 and 5.4, and Lemma 5.2. The algorithms and codes may be constructed over any field; however, since systems predominately use binary codes, we concentrate on constructions over GF(2).

(3) The new decoding procedure for this class of codes is based on Lemma 5.1 and Theorem 5.1. Due to the inherent concurrency of the decoding algorithm described in Section 5.2 and illustrated in Figure 5.1, the decoder design can be realised using parallel architecture.

(4) It is demonstrated in Section 5.4 that these codes can be used to provide adaptive error correction. This property is used to describe a novel generalised hybrid automatic repeat request scheme which incorporates such codes for error correction. This scheme is described in Sections 7.1 and 7.3, and it is established in Section 7.5 that the proposed generalisation results in high throughput (Figures 7.7 and 7.8) even during poor channel conditions.

1.2 Plan of the Monograph

The monograph is divided into two parts; Part I contains four
chapters and is an indepth study of the relationship between the
computation of bilinear forms and the linear error-correcting codes.
Part II contains two chapters and describes an application of the class
of linear codes obtained in Part I, for providing adaptive error -
correction in digital communication systems. A brief description of the
chapters follows.

In Chapter 2, we study the multiplicative complexity of certain
noncommutative algorithms that may be used to compute a system of k
bilinear forms and establish a connection between linear (n,k,d) codes
and the algorithms. A particular system of bilinear forms is considered
and by using the property of duality, it is shown that the
multiplicative complexity of the bilinear form is the same as the
multiplicative complexity of a length (k+d-1) aperiodic convolution
algorithm.

In Chapter 3, efficient algorithms for aperiodic convolutions are
developed. Two approaches for aperiodic convolution are described; the
first approach reduces the problem of computing a large length aperiodic
convolution to a number of small length aperiodic convolutions using the
Chinese Remainder Theorem (CRT), while the second approach consists in
converting a one-dimensional aperiodic convolution into multidimensional
aperiodic convolutions. It is worthwhile to mention here that the
emphasis in this work is on the first approach and the related class of
linear codes.

In Chapter 4, bilinear algorithms for aperiodic convolution of
sequences defined over GF(2) and GF(3), and the corresponding linear

error-correcting codes are derived. These algorithms are based on the two approaches developed in Chapter 3. Knowledge concerning the field of constants is incorporated in the design of the algorithms. As the binary codes are most extensively used in present-day systems, the emphasis in the monograph is on the study of binary linear codes and their properties. Some of the unique features of this new class of codes are also illustrated in this chapter.

In Chapter 5, we present the decoding procedure for the class of codes obtained from the aperiodic convolution algorithms developed in the previous chapters. This decoding procedure possesses certain unique features which are also highlighted in the sequel. It is established that the length and the error-correcting capability of these codes can be varied easily, and consequently, the encoder/decoder can be designed to incorporate a large number of these codes into a single configuration.

Chapter 6 is a brief introduction to the basic automatic repeat request (ARQ) schemes and their retransmission protocols. It also dwells on the problem of the throughput of ARQ systems for high error rate channels and we describe two types of hybrid ARQ techniques that can be used to combat such a problem.

The type-II hybrid ARQ scheme of Chapter 6 is generalised in Chapter 7. This scheme is termed the GH-ARQ technique. It is demonstrated that the class of codes derived in Chapters 4 and 5 can be used in GH-ARQ systems to provide high throughput for communication over channels having non-stationary characteristics. Finally, the GH-ARQ scheme is analysed with respect to the two important measures of performance for ARQ systems.

In Chapter 8, the conclusions of the work are presented.

We hope that this research work will provide impetus, motivation, and stimulation to a future researcher to explore further the computational complexity aspects of bilinear forms, their relationships to algebraic coding theory, and the applications of the resulting classes of codes to digital communications systems.

PART I

COMPUTATIONAL COMPLEXITY OF

BILINEAR FORMS AND RELATION TO

ALGEBRAIC CODING THEORY

CHAPTER 2

BILINEAR FORMS AND LINEAR CODES

The mathematical preliminaries fundamental to the content of this work are presented in this chapter. The multiplicative complexity of a system of bilinear forms is defined and a number of useful results relating the system to linear error-correcting codes are described. A particular bilinear form is considered and it is shown that its computation can be performed as an aperiodic convolution.

The correspondence between linear (n,k,d) codes and algorithms for computing a system ψ of k bilinear forms was first studied by Lempel et al [5]. This correspondence indicates that the codeword length, n, is equal to the multiplicative complexity of the algorithm used for computing the system ψ and, further, that the minimum distance of the code, d, is lowerbounded by the minimum number of multiplications required to compute any linear combination of k forms in the bilinear system. In the previous work, specific bilinear forms associated with Bose-Chaudhary-Hocquenghem (BCH) and Reed-Solomon (RS) codes were described along with an unconventional procedure for a part of the decoding process. In other work along these lines, the connection between algorithms used for computing systems of bilinear forms and binary linear codes has been observed by Brockett et al [16].

2.1 Mathematical Preliminaries

In the field of arithmetic complexity, algebraic problems such as function evaluation are analysed to determine the number of arithmetic operations required by an algorithm. Let F be a given field and $x_1, x_2, \ldots, x_r$ be indeterminates over F. The extension of F, denoted by

$F[x_1, x_2, \ldots, x_r]$, is the smallest commutative ring R such that R contains $F \cup \{x_1, x_2, \ldots, x_r\}$. The model of computation we employ is the **straight line program model**, wherein a computation consists of a sequence of instructions of the type

$$f_i \leftarrow g_i \ominus h_i$$

where $\ominus$ is one of the operations $+$, $-$ or $\times$; f_i is a variable not appearing in any previous step; and g_i and h_i are either indeterminates, elements of F, or variable names appearing on the left of the arrow at a previous step. An element of F appearing in a computation is called a constant. A computation computes E, a set of expressions in $F[x_1, x_2, \ldots, x_r]$, with respect to F if for each expression e in E, there is some variable f in the computation such that the value of f = e. The **multiplicative complexity** of an expression e is defined as the minimum number of instructions of the specific type $f_i \leftarrow g_i \times h_i$ required to compute e, where instructions involving multiplications by constants are not included [17].

2.2 Multiplicative Complexity of Bilinear Forms and Linear Codes

Here we consider the problem of computing a system ψ of k bilinear forms which can be formulated in terms of computing the product of a matrix X and a column vector $\underline{y}$. Thus, the problem may be represented as,

$$\psi = X\underline{y}$$

The elements of the matrix X are linear forms of the type $\sum_{i=1}^{r} a_i x_i$, $a_i \in F$, in the indeterminates $x_1, x_2, \ldots, x_r$ and $\underline{y}$ is a column vector $(y_1 y_2 \cdots y_s)^T$. Here, T denotes matrix transposition.

It is well known that without division, bilinear forms can be computed as linear combinations of products of pairs of linear forms in the indeterminates [18]. An **algorithm** to compute ψ is an expression of the form,

$$C(A\underline{x} \times B\underline{y}),$$

where A,B,C are matrices of dimensions (n×r), (n×s), and (k×n), respectively, over F; $\underline{x}$ is the column vector $(x_1 x_2 \cdots x_r)^T$; and × denotes a component-by-component multiplication of vectors. The algorithm $C(A\underline{x} \times B\underline{y})$ for computing X$\underline{y}$ is said to be noncommutative (NC). Since the straightline program model of evaluating $C(A\underline{x} \times B\underline{y})$ requires n multiplications, the multiplicative complexity of the algorithm is n. We now state various results that establish: (i) the lower bound for the multiplicative complexity of the algorithms used to compute the system of bilinear forms, and (ii) the connection between the bilinear forms and linear (n,k,d) codes over an arbitrary finite field F. The reader is referred to [18] and [5] for more detailed description and proofs.

Definition. Let $F^m[x_1, x_2, \ldots, x_r]$ be the m-dimensional vector space with components from $F[x_1, x_2, \ldots, x_r]$, and F^m be the m-dimensional vector space with components from F. A set of vectors $\{\underline{v}_1, \ldots, \underline{v}_\alpha\}$ from $F^m[x_1, x_2, \ldots, x_r]$ is linearly independent modulo F^m, if for $a_1, a_2, \ldots, a_\alpha$ in F, $\sum_{i=1}^{\alpha} a_i \underline{v}_i$ in F^m implies that all the a_i are zero. The row rank of a (k×s) matrix X modulo F^s (referred to as row rank of X in the sequel) is the number of lienarly independent rows of X modulo F^s. The column rank of X modulo F^k is defined analogously. ∎

Theorem 2.1. (A row-oriented lower bound on multiplications)

Let X$\underline{y}$ be a system of bilinear forms over F. If the row rank of X

is α (over F), then any computation of $X\underline{y}$ requires at least α
multiplications. ∎

<u>Theorem 2.2</u>. (A column-oriented lower bound on multiplications)

Let $X\underline{y}$ be a system of bilinear forms over F. If the column rank of
X is β (over F), then any computation of $X\underline{y}$ requires at least β
multiplications. ∎

<u>Theorem 2.3</u>. (A row <u>and</u> column oriented bound on multiplications)

Let $X\underline{y}$ be a system of bilinear forms over F. If X has a submatrix
W with α rows and β columns such that for any vectors $\underline{u}$ and $\underline{v}$ in F^{α} and
F^{β}, respectively, $\underline{u}^T W \underline{v}$ is an element of F if and only if (<u>iff</u>) either
$\underline{u} = \underline{0}$ or $\underline{v} = \underline{0}$, then any computation of $X\underline{y}$ requires at least $(\alpha+\beta-1)$
multiplications. ∎

Let μ be the minimum number of multiplications required to compute
a system ψ of k bilinear forms. Then, for any integer $n \geqslant \mu$, a
computation of ψ can be expressed as $C(A\underline{x} \times B\underline{y})$, where A, B, and C are
matrices of dimensions $(n\times r)$, $(n\times s)$, and $(k\times n)$, respectively, over F.
If the row rank of X, $\rho(x)$, is k, then by Theorem 2.1, $n \geqslant k$ and the
rank of C is k. The matrix C can be treated as the <u>generator</u> <u>matrix</u> of
a linear (n,k) code over F. A typical codeword $\underline{c}^T$ is $\underline{a}^T C$, where $\underline{a}$ is a
k-dimensional column vector of information symbols. Since the bilinear
form $\underline{a}^T X \underline{y} = \underline{a}^T C(A\underline{x} \times B\underline{y})$, we see that the weight (number of nonzero
components) of $\underline{c}$ cannot be less than the multiplicative complexity of
the bilinear form $\underline{a}^T X \underline{y}$, which by Theorem 2.2, is not less than $\rho(\underline{a}^T X)$,
the row rank of $\underline{a}^T X$. Hence, we state the following theorem [5]:

<u>Theorem 2.4</u>. Given a system $\psi = X\underline{y}$ of k linearly independent bilinear
forms, for every computation of the form $\psi = C(A\underline{x} \times B\underline{y})$, the $(k\times n)$ matrix
C generates a linear $(n,k,\bar{d})$ code over F, where

$$\bar{d} \geqslant d = \min_{\underline{a} \in F^k} \{\rho(\underline{a}^T X)\} \ , \quad \underline{a} \neq \underline{0}$$

Here, d is the design distance of the linear code and $\bar{d}$ is the actual minimum distance of the code generated. ∎

2.3 Dual of a Bilinear Form

Let $\underline{z}$ be the column vector $(z_1 z_2 \cdots z_k)^T$ and $C(A\underline{x} \times B\underline{y})$ be a computation of ψ. The P-dual of the computation is the computation $A^T(C^T\underline{z} \times B\underline{y})$; the R-dual of the computation is the computation $B^T(A\underline{x} \times C^T\underline{z})$. The procedure employed to obtain the dual for a given computation for a system of bilinear forms is described in [5]. In this connection, the following theorem is also of interest to us in this work [18].

<u>Theorem 2.5.</u> There is a computation for the system of expressions represented by $C(A\underline{x} \times B\underline{y})$ having n multiplications <u>iff</u> there is a computation having n multiplications for its P-dual $A^T(C^T\underline{z} \times B\underline{y})$; its R-dual $B^T(A\underline{x} \times C^T\underline{z})$; the vector reversed system of expressions $C(B\underline{y} \times A\underline{x})$; and the vector reversed system of expressions for the P-dual and R-dual represented by $A^T(B\underline{y} \times C^T\underline{z})$ and $B^T(C^T\underline{z} \times A\underline{x})$, respectively. ∎

2.4 A Particular Bilinear Form

Let us consider the computation of a system ψ of k bilinear forms given by,

$$\psi = X\underline{y} = \begin{bmatrix} x_0 & x_1 & x_2 & \cdots & x_{d-2} & x_{d-1} \\ x_1 & x_2 & x_3 & \cdots & x_{d-1} & x_d \\ x_2 & x_3 & x_4 & \cdots & \cdot & \cdot \\ \vdots & \vdots & \vdots & & \vdots & \vdots \\ x_{k-1} & x_k & x_{k+1} & \cdots & x_{k+d-3} & x_{k+d-2} \end{bmatrix} \begin{bmatrix} y_0 \\ y_1 \\ \vdots \\ y_{d-1} \end{bmatrix} \quad (2.1)$$

It can be easily shown for the above form of X, that for $\forall \underline{a} \in F^k$, $\underline{a} \neq \underline{0}$ and $\forall \underline{b} \in F^d$, $\underline{b} \neq \underline{0}$, we have $\underline{a}^T X \underline{b} \neq 0$; therefore, $\rho(\underline{a}^T X) = d$ for all nonzero $\underline{a} \in F^k$. Hence, if $C(A\underline{x} \times B\underline{y})$ is a computation of such a system of bilinear forms, then C generates an $(n,k,\bar{d})$ linear code over F with $\bar{d} \geqslant d$, where n is the multiplicative complexity of the computation $C(A\underline{x} \times B\underline{y})$, which by Theorem 2.3, is at least $k+d-1$. If the actual multiplicative complexity of the computation, n, is equal to the theoretical lowerbound given by $k+d-1$, i.e., if $n = k+d-1$, then the corresponding linear codes are referred to as maximum-distance-separable codes [9].

In order to derive an algorithm for computing the system (2.1), we consider the P-dual Φ of the above computation, $A^T(C^T\underline{z} \times B\underline{y})$, where $\underline{z}$ is a column vector given by $(z_0 z_1 \cdots z_{k-1})^T$. It is observed that such a computation corresponds to the following lower triangular system of bilinear forms,

$$
\Phi = Z\underline{y} =
\begin{bmatrix}
z_0 & 0 & 0 & \cdots & 0 & 0 \\
z_1 & z_0 & 0 & & & \vdots \\
z_2 & z_1 & z_0 & \cdots & 0 & \\
\vdots & \vdots & & & z_0 & 0 \\
z_{k-1} & & & & & \vdots \\
0 & z_{k-1} & & \cdots & z_{k-1} & z_0 \\
\vdots & \vdots & & & & \vdots \\
0 & 0 & \cdots & \cdots & 0 & z_{k-1}
\end{bmatrix}
\begin{bmatrix}
y_0 \\
y_1 \\
\vdots \\
y_{d-1}
\end{bmatrix}.
\tag{2.2}
$$

Here Φ is a column vector of bilinear forms $(\phi_0 \ \phi_1 \ \cdots \ \phi_{N-1})^T$ of length N, where $N = k+d-1$. From the structure of the system given in (2.2), it is clear that the ϕ_i, $i = 0,1,\ldots,$ N-1 can be considered as the simple aperiodic convolution of two sequences, z_j, $j = 0,1,\ldots,$ k-1 of length k and y_ℓ, $\ell = 0,1,\ldots,$ d-1 of length d, i.e.,

$$\phi_i = \sum_{\substack{0 \leqslant j \leqslant k-1 \\ 0 \leqslant \ell \leqslant d-1 \\ j+\ell=i}} z_j \, y_\ell \qquad i = 0, 1, \ldots, N-1. \qquad (2.3)$$

Let us define the generating polynomial of the sequence z_j, $j = 0,1,\ldots,$ k-1 by $Z(u) = \sum_{j=0}^{k-1} z_j u^j$. We assume similar definitions for $Y(u)$ and $\Phi(u)$, the generating polynomials of the sequences y_ℓ, and ϕ_i, respectively. It is easily seen that $\Phi(u) = Z(u)Y(u)$. Therefore, the dual bilinear form can be computed as a polynomial product. We summarise this discussion in the following manner.

The linear codes generated from the computation $C(A\underline{x} \times B\underline{y})$ of the system of bilinear forms defined by (2.1), have the parameters $(n,k,\bar{d})$, where n is the multiplicative complexity of the aperiodic convolution algorithm of length $N = k+d-1$, and $\bar{d} \geqslant d$. Note that if the multiplicative complexity of the algorithm to compute the dual of a computation is n, then it follows from Theorem 2.5 that the multiplicative complexity of the computation itself is also n. If the aperiodic convolution is computed as $\Phi = P(Q\underline{z} \times R\underline{y})$, then by comparing the expression for the dual to the computation $C(A\underline{x} \times B\underline{y})$, we obtain the generator matrix of the linear code as $C = Q^T$.

Using the property that over a field F having at least N-1 elements, the multiplicative complexity of an aperiodic convolution of length N expressed as $Z(u)Y(u)$ is N, RS codes have been derived over $GF(p^m)$ in [5]. In the following chapters, we discuss the design of efficient algorithms for computing the aperiodic convolution over an arbitrary finite field using the Chinese remainder theorem and multidimensional convolution techniques and generating the associated class of linear codes.

CHAPTER 3

EFFICIENT ALGORITHMS FOR THE APERIODIC CONVOLUTION

OF SEQUENCES

In this chapter, we develop efficient algorithms for the aperiodic
convolution of two sequences. Since the multiplicative complexity of
the aperiodic convolution also determines the length of the linear
codes, a worthwhile objective is to develop efficient algorithms with as
low a multiplicative complexity as possible.

Let us consider the aperiodic convolution of two sequences
z_j, $j = 0,1,\ldots,k-1$ and y_ℓ, $\ell = 0,1,\ldots,d-1$ as the polynomial product
$\Phi(u) = Z(u)Y(u)$, where $\Phi(u)$, $Z(u)$, and $Y(u)$ are the generating
polynomials of the corresponding sequences. There are two techniques
that can be used to compute such a product: the first technique
represents a large degree polynomial product as a number of small degree
polynomial products and the second technique converts a one-dimensional
polynomial product into multidimensional polynomial products. The
Chinese remainder theorem plays a central role in the computation of
convolutions and we begin this chapter by describing the theorem.

3.1   Chinese Remainder Theorem for Polynomials

Let a polynomial $P(u)$ be the product of t relatively prime
polynomials $P_i(u)$, $i = 1,2,\ldots,t$, that is, $P(u) = \prod_{i=1}^{t} P_i(u)$. Two
polynomials $P_i(u)$ and $P_j(u)$ are relatively prime if they have no common
polynomial factors. Then, in the ring of polynomials modulo $P(u)$, the
polynomial $Y(u)$ can be expressed uniquely as a function of the
polynomials $Y_i(u)$, obtained by reducing $Y(u)$ modulo the polynomials

$P_i(u)$, $i = 1,2,\ldots,t$. The Chinese remainder theorem for polynomials (CRT) can be expressed as,

$$Y(u) \equiv \sum_{i=1}^{t} S_i(u)Y_i(u) \text{ modulo } P(u), \qquad (3.1)$$

where the polynomials $S_i(u)$ satisfy the following congruences,

$$S_i(u) \equiv \begin{cases} 0 & \text{modulo } P_j(u), \; j=1,2,\ldots,t; \quad j \neq i \\ 1 & \text{modulo } P_i(u) \end{cases} \qquad (3.2)$$

The polynomials $S_i(u)$ have the form,

$$S_i(u) = R_i(u) \prod_{\substack{j=1 \\ j \neq i}}^{t} P_j(u),$$

where the polynomials $R_i(u)$ are determined from the single congruence,

$$R_i(u) \prod_{\substack{j=1 \\ j \neq i}}^{t} P_j(u) \equiv 1 \quad \text{modulo } P_i(u) \qquad (3.3)$$

The Chinese remainder theorem may be proved by reducing (3.1) modulo the various polynomials $P_i(u)$ to obtain the condition expressed in (3.2). Since each of the polynomials $P_i(u)$ is relatively prime to all the other polynomials $P_j(u)$, $j \neq i$, $P_i(u)$ has an inverse modulo every other polynomial. Such a constraint is essential on the forms of the polynomials $P_i(u)$ for the existence of the polynomials $R_i(u)$ that satisfy (3.3). The problem of computing the polynomials $R_i(u)$ is the polynomial equivalent of the diophantine equation, and is solved by use of Euclid's algorithm [12].

3.2 Convolution Algorithms Based on the CRT

We begin this section by describing a basic procedure to compute the aperiodic convolution as a polynomial product.

3.2.1 Basic procedure

Consider the polynomial product,

$$\Phi(u) = Z(u)Y(u) \tag{3.4}$$

where the polynomials $Z(u)$ and $Y(u)$ are of degree k-1 and d-1, respectively. The degree of the polynomial $\Phi(u)$, therefore, is k+d-2. Let N = k+d-1. Since $\Phi(u)$ is of degree N-1, $\Phi(u)$ is unchanged if it is defined modulo any polynomial P(u) of degree at least N, that is,

$$\Phi(u) \equiv Z(u)Y(u) \text{ modulo } P(u), \ \deg[P(u)] \geqslant N \tag{3.5}$$

If P(u) is the product of t relatively prime polynomials $P_i(u)$, i=1,2,...,t, that is, $P(u) = \prod_{i=1}^{t} P_i(u)$, then $\Phi(u)$ can be computed by first reducing the polynomials $Z(u)$ and $Y(u)$ modulo $P_i(u)$,

$$Z_i(u) \equiv Z(u) \text{ modulo } P_i(u)$$
$$i = 1,2,...,t \tag{3.6}$$
$$Y_i(u) \equiv Y(u) \text{ modulo } P_i(u)$$

The polynomial $\Phi(u)$ is obtained by computing the t polynomial products,

$$\Phi_i(u) \equiv Z_i(u)Y_i(u) \text{ modulo } P_i(u),$$

and, then, using the CRT to uniquely reconstruct $\Phi(u)$ from the products modulo $P_i(u)$.

3.2.2 Complexity of the basic procedure

If $M(\alpha_i)$ denotes the number of multiplications required to calculate the ith polynomial product $\Phi_i(u) \equiv Z_i(u)Y_i(u)$ modulo $P_i(u)$, where $\deg[P_i(u)] = \alpha_i$, then the multiplicative complexity of the procedure, and consequently, the length n of the linear code generated is,

$$n = M(N) = \sum_{i=1}^{t} M(\alpha_i) \qquad (3.7)$$

Note that the multiplicative complexity is denoted by $M(\alpha_i)$ for convenience; however, the complexity depends on the precise form of $P_i(u)$.

As was stated earlier, the objective is to develop algorithms with as low a multiplicative complexity as possible for given values of k and d. Therefore for a given degree D, of the polynomial P(u), the factors $P_i(u)$ are selected in such a way that the multiplicative complexity of the computation Z(u)Y(u) modulo P(u) is as low as possible. In general, a large number of relatively prime polynomial factors leads to a computationally efficient procedure. With this in mind, the following criteria should be satisfied:

(i) $P_i(u)$ and $P_j(u)$ relatively prime $1 \leqslant i \leqslant j \leqslant t$; $i \neq j$,

(ii) $\sum_{i=1}^{t} \deg [P_i(u)] = \deg [P(u)] = D$, and

(iii) Each of the polynomials $P_i(u)$ have as low a degree as possible.

Note that the form of the polynomials $P_i(u)$ depends on the field of constants, F. For example, there are two distinct polynomials of degree one defined over GF(2), u and (u+1), while there are three distinct polynomials of degree one defined over GF(3), u,(u+1), and (u+2). Thus, knowledge about the field of constants is incorporated directly into the design of the algorithm.

3.2.3 Improvements in the basic procedure

The multiplicative complexity of the algorithm can be further reduced by suitably modifying the above described basic procedure to permit intentional wraparound of the polynomial coefficients. For example, if $M(N-1) < M(N)-1$, then it is more efficient to calculate $\Phi(u)$ from the product $Z(u)Y(u)$ modulo $P'(u)$, where $\deg[P'(u)] = N-1$, with one extra multiplication, i.e., $z_{k-1} \cdot y_{d-1}$. Similarly, if $M(N-2) < M(N-1)-2 < M(N)-3$, it may be preferable to compute $\Phi(u)$ from the product $Z(u)Y(u)$ modulo $P''(u)$, where $\deg[P''(u)] = N-2$, with three more multiplications. Also, if $P_i(u)$ is of the form $(u-a_i)^{\alpha_i}$, where $a_i \in F$, the product $Z_i(u)Y_i(u)$ modulo $(u-a_i)^{\alpha_i}$ is relatively less complex to compute, in general, as compared to $Z_i(u)Y_i(u)$ for several values of α_i. The modified algorithm to compute the product $Z(u)Y(u)$ can be described in three schemes, as given below:

Scheme 1. Computation of $Z(u)Y(u)$, $\deg[Z(u)] = k-1$, $\deg[Y(u)] = d-1$. If $k = d = 1$, the result is obtained in one multiplication; otherwise, select an integer s so as to minimise the total number of multiplications required to compute,

    (i) $Z(u)Y(u)$ modulo $P(u)$, $\deg[P(u)] = N-s$, and

    (ii) $\bar{Z}(u)\bar{Y}(u)$ modulo u^s using scheme 3, where

$$\bar{Z}(u) = Z(u^{-1})u^{k-1} \text{ and } \bar{Y}(u) = Y(u^{-1})u^{d-1}.$$

Scheme 2. Computation of $Z_i(u)Y_i(u)$ modulo $P_i(u)$. If $P_i(u) = (u-a_i)^{\alpha_i}$, where $a_i \in F$, use Scheme 3 to compute $Z_i(u)Y_i(u)$ modulo $P_i(u)$; otherwise, compute the ordinary product $Z_i(u)Y_i(u)$ and reduce modulo $P_i(u)$.

Scheme 3. Computation of $Z_i(u)Y_i(u)$ modulo $P_i(u)$, $P_i(u) = (u-a_i)^{\alpha_i}$,

$a_i \in F$. If $a_i = 0$, use one of the following two methods which is least

computationally complex, in terms of multiplicative complexity:

(i) Use Scheme 2.

(ii) Let $Z_i(u) = z_0' + z_1'u + \cdots + z_{\alpha_i-1}'u^{\alpha_i-1}$ and $Y_i(u) =$

$y_0' + y_1'u + \cdots + y_{\alpha_i-1}'u^{\alpha_i-1}$ and define $m_{\ell_1\ell_2} = (\sum_{e=\ell_1}^{\ell_2} z_e')(\sum_{f=\ell_1}^{\ell_2} y_f')$,

then we have

$$z_{\ell_1}'y_{\ell_2}' + z_{\ell_2}'y_{\ell_1}' = m_{\ell_1\ell_2} + m_{\ell_1+1,\ell_2-1} - m_{\ell_1,\ell_2-1} - m_{\ell_1+1,\ell_2}$$

It can be shown that the number of multiplications required to

obtain the product $Z_i(u)Y_i(u)$ modulo $P_i(u)$ is given by $\beta(\beta+1)-1$ for

$\alpha_i = 2\beta-1$ and $\beta(\beta+2)$ for $\alpha_i = 2\beta$ [19].

If $a_i \neq 0$, define $\tilde{Z}_i(u) = Z_i(u+a_i)$ and $\tilde{Y}_i(u) = Y_i(u+a_i)$ and

compute $\tilde{\Phi}_i(u) = \tilde{Z}_i(u)\tilde{Y}_i(u)$ modulo u^{α_i} as described above. The product

$\Phi_i(u)$ is then given by $\Phi_i(u) = \tilde{\Phi}_i(u-a_i)$.

By using bilinear small degree polynomial multiplication

algorithms, some of which are given in Appendix A, and the procedure

described above, we can design bilinear algorithms for larger values of

N. Such a procedure is quite straightforward and requires no further

elaboration.

In the next chapter, several examples of algorithms for aperiodic

convolution and the corresponding binary linear codes generated are

presented. The various properties of such a family of codes are also

described.

3.3   <u>Multidimensional Convolution Algorithms</u>

In multidimensional convolution technique, the one-dimensional polynomial product is computed by converting it into a multidimensional polynomial product. This technique can alternatively be interpreted as an algorithm that uses small degree polynomial products recursively to compute the product of large degree polynomials. The aperiodic convolution algorithm based on the CRT (described in the previous section) and the multidimensional convolution algorithm (described in the following) may be compared in terms of the associated multiplicative complexity. For a given value of k and d, the algorithm having the smaller multiplicative complexity is preferred for reasons discussed earlier. Let us assume that we want to compute the polynomial product,

$$\Phi(u) = Z(u)Y(u)$$

where $\Phi(u) = \sum_{i=0}^{N-1} \phi_i u^i$,

$$Z(u) = \sum_{j=0}^{k-1} z_j u^j,$$

and $Y(u) = \sum_{\ell=0}^{d-1} y_\ell u^\ell$.

Let k and d be composite numbers having a common factor, that is, k and d have the form $k = k_1 c$ and $d = d_1 c$. Then $Z(u)Y(u)$ may be transformed into a two-dimensional polynomial product in the following manner. Define the quantities,

$$j = cj_2 + j_1, \quad j_2 = 0, 1, \ldots, k_1 - 1; \quad \ell_1, \; j_1 = 0, 1, \ldots, c-1$$

$$\ell = c\ell_2 + \ell_1, \quad \ell_2 = 0, 1, \ldots, d_1 - 1$$

$$u_1 = u^c$$

and let $Z(u, u_1)$, $Y(u, u_1)$ and $\Phi(u, u_1)$ denote the two-dimensional polynomials corresponding to the polynomials $Z(u)$, $Y(u)$, and $\Phi(u)$, respectively. Using the above, the polynomials $Z(u, u_1)$ and $Y(u, u_1)$ can be expressed as,

$$Z(u) = Z(u, u_1) = \sum_{j_1 = 0}^{c-1} Z_{j_1}(u_1) \, u^{j_1},$$

and

$$Y(u) = Y(u, u_1) = \sum_{\ell_1 = 0}^{c-1} Y_{\ell_1}(u_1) \, u^{\ell_1},$$

where

$$Z_{j_1}(u_1) = \sum_{j_2 = 0}^{k_1 - 1} z_{cj_2 + j_1} \, u_1^{j_2},$$

and

$$Y_{\ell_1}(u_1) = \sum_{\ell_2 = 0}^{d_1 - 1} y_{c\ell_2 + \ell_1} \, u_1^{\ell_2}.$$

Thus, $Z(u, u_1)$ is a $(c-1)$ degree polynomial in u, where each coefficient, in turn, is a polynomial of degree $(k_1 - 1)$ in u_1. Similarly, $Y(u, u_1)$ is a $(c-1)$ degree polynomial in u, where each coefficient, in turn, is a polynomial of degree $(d_1 - 1)$ in u_1. The product of $Z(u, u_1)$ and $Y(u, u_1)$ is a two-dimensional polynomial $\Phi(u, u_1)$, and is given by,

$$\Phi(u, u_1) = \sum_{\ell_1 = 0}^{c-1} \sum_{j_1 = 0}^{c-1} Z_{j_1}(u) Y_{\ell_1}(u) \, u^{j_1 + \ell_1}. \tag{3.8}$$

The polynomial $\Phi(u)$ may be obtained from $\Phi(u, u_1)$ simply by replacing u_1 by u^c. It is clear from (3.8) that $\Phi(u, u_1)$ is computed as the product

of two polynomials, each of degree $(c-1)$, in which every multiplication
is replaced by the product of two polynomials of degrees (k_1-1) and
(d_1-1). Let n_1 be the number of multiplications required to compute the
product of two polynomials of degrees (k_1-1) and (d_1-1), and n_2 be the
number of multiplications required to compute the product of two
polynomials each of degree $(c-1)$. Hence, the product of two polynomials
of degrees $(k-1)$ and $(d-1)$ is computed in n multiplications, using
(3.8), where

$$n = n_1 n_2.$$

The above described two-dimensional approach can easily be
extended to obtain m-dimensional $(m > 2)$ convolution algorithms. It is
worthwhile to mention here that this approach is also based on
computations of products of small degree polynomials. However, in order
to convert a one-dimensional polynomial product into a multidimensional
polynomial product, the lengths of the polynomials must be composite
with a common factor. Such a constraint restricts the applicability of
this approach to the generation of linear codes. For example, 3, 5 and
7 have no composite factors and, consequently, this approach cannot be
employed if any one of k or d is equal to 3, 5, or 7.

CHAPTER 4

A NEW CLASS OF LINEAR CODES

In this chapter, we develop algorithms for aperiodic convolution over the finite field of interest and the related class of codes. As the binary codes are most extensively used in systems employing error-correcting codes, the emphasis in this chapter is on the study of binary linear codes and their properties. We begin this chapter by deriving binary linear codes obtained from aperiodic convolution algorithms based on the CRT. Such a class of linear codes possesses a number of interesting properties that can be used in digital communication systems. A shift-register based implementation for the encoding procedure is also given. Finally, linear codes defined over GF(3) and linear codes obtained from the multidimensional convolution algorithms are also described.

4.1 CRT-Based Convolution Algorithms Over GF(2) and Related Codes

Given below is a list of certain polynomials over GF(2) of degree less than 6,

degree 1: $\quad u, u+1$

degree 2: $\quad u^2, u^2+1, u^2+u+1$

degree 3: $\quad u^3, u^3+u^2+u+1, u^3+u+1, u^3+u^2+1$

degree 4: $\quad u^4, u^4+1, u^4+u^2+1, u^4+u+1, u^4+u^3+u^2+u+1, u^4+u^3+1$

degree 5: $\quad u^5, u^5+u^4+u+1, u^5+u^2+1, u^5+u^4+u^3+u^2+1, u^5+u^4+u^2+u+1,$
$\quad\quad\quad\quad u^5+u^3+u^2+u+1, u^5+u^4+u^3+u+1, u^5+u^3+1$

For each degree i, only those polynomials are listed which are not products of two distinct polynomials of lower degree. For example, (u^3+u^2) is not listed as a degree 3 polynomial; this is to help in the choice of the polynomial P(u) as a product of relatively prime polynomials $P_i(u)$, i = 1,...,t. For a given degree of the polynomial P(u), its factors are selected in such a way that the multiplicative complexity of the computation Z(u)Y(u) modulo P(u) is as low as possible.

For example, given below is the list of polynomials of degree up to 15 obtained by selecting the appropriate polynomials from the list and arranging them in the manner described in Section 3.2,

D = 3: $P(u) = (u+1)(u^2+u+1)$

D = 4: $P(u) = u(u+1)(u^2+u+1)$

D = 5: $P(u) = u(u^2+1)(u^2+u+1)$

D = 6: $P(u) = u^2(u^2+1)(u^2+u+1)$

D = 7: $P(u) = u(u+1)(u^2+u+1)(u^3+u^2+1)$

D = 8: $P(u) = u(u^2+1)(u^2+u+1)(u^3+u^2+1)$

D = 9: $P(u) = u^2(u^2+1)(u^2+u+1)(u^3+u^2+1)$

D = 10: $P(u) = u(u+1)(u^2+u+1)(u^3+u+1)(u^3+u^2+1)$

D = 11: $P(u) = u(u^2+1)(u^2+u+1)(u^3+u+1)(u^3+u^2+1)$

D = 12: $P(u) = u^2(u^2+1)(u^2+u+1)(u^3+u+1)(u^3+u^2+1)$

D = 13: $P(u) = u^3(u^2+1)(u^2+u+1)(u^3+u+1)(u^3+u^2+1)$

D = 14: $P(u) = u^3(u^3+u^2+u+1)(u^2+u+1)(u^3+u+1)(u^3+u^2+1)$

D = 15: $P(u) = u(u^2+1)(u^2+u+1)(u^3+u+1)(u^3+u^2+1)(u^4+u+1)$

Note that the choice of the polynomial P(u) is not unique for a given degree D. For example, for D = 5, P(u) can have either one of the two forms, $P(u) = u^2(u+1)(u^2+u+1)$ or $P(u) = u(u^2+1)(u^2+u+1)$. However, the multiplicative complexity of the procedure Z(u)Y(u) modulo P(u) is the

same for all such choices. In the following, we derive bilinear
convolution algorithms of length 6 and 16 and the corresponding binary
codes.

4.1.1 Bilinear convolution algorithm of length 6 and the corresponding
    code

Since $N = k+d-1 = 6$, we have $k+d = 7$. Let $d = 3$ and $k = 4$.
Therefore, $Z(u) = z_0 + z_1 u + z_2 u^2 + z_3 u^3$ and $Y(u) = y_0 + y_1 u + y_2 u^2$. We choose
$P(u) = u(u^2+1)(u^2+u+1)$ and $s = 1$, to compute the aperiodic convolution
$\Phi(u) = Z(u)Y(u)$. Let $P_1(u) = u$, $P_2(u) = (u^2+1)$, and $P_3(u) = (u^2+u+1)$.
Reducing the polynomials $Z(u)$ and $Y(u)$ modulo each of $P_i(u)$, we obtain

$$Z_1(u) \equiv Z(u) \text{ modulo } u$$

$$= z_0$$

$$Y_1(u) \equiv Y(u) \text{ modulo } u$$

$$= y_0.$$

Let $m_0 = z_0 \cdot y_0$. Then $\Phi_1(u) \equiv \Phi(u)$ modulo u is equal to m_0. Similarly,

$$Z_2(u) \equiv Z(u) \text{ modulo } (u^2+1)$$

$$= (z_0+z_2) + (z_1+z_3)u$$

$$Y_2(u) \equiv Y(u) \text{ modulo } (u^2+1)$$

$$= (y_0+y_2) + y_1 u.$$

Let,

$$m_1 = (z_0+z_2) \cdot (y_0+y_2)$$

$$m_2 = (z_0+z_1+z_2+z_3) \cdot (y_0+y_1+y_2)$$

$$m_3 = (z_1+z_3) \cdot y_1$$

then,

$$\Phi_2(u) \equiv \Phi(u) \text{ modulo } (u^2+1)$$

$$= (m_1 + m_3) + (m_1 + m_2 + m_3)u.$$

Also,
$$Z_3(u) \equiv Z(u) \text{ modulo } (u^2 + u + 1)$$

$$= (z_0 + z_2 + z_3) + (z_1 + z_2)u$$

$$Y_3(u) \equiv Y(u) \text{ modulo } (u^2 + u + 1)$$

$$= (y_0 + y_2) + (y_1 + y_2)u.$$

Let,
$$m_4 = (z_0 + z_2 + z_3) \cdot (y_0 + y_2)$$

$$m_5 = (z_0 + z_1 + z_3) \cdot (y_0 + y_1)$$

$$m_6 = (z_1 + z_2) \cdot (y_1 + y_2)$$

then,
$$\Phi_3(u) \equiv \Phi(u) \text{ modulo } (u^2 + u + 1)$$

$$= (m_4 + m_6) + (m_4 + m_5)u.$$

The polynomial $\Phi(u)$ modulo $P(u)$ can be recovered from the polynomials $\Phi_i(u)$, $i = 1, 2, 3$, using the CRT,

$$\Phi(u) \equiv \sum_{i=1}^{3} S_i(u)\Phi_i(u) \text{ modulo } P(u).$$

The polynomials $S_i(u)$, $i = 1, 2, 3$ are found to be $S_1(u) = (u^4 + u^3 + u + 1)$, $S_2(u) = (u^3 + u^2 + u)$, and $S_3(u) = (u^4 + u^2)$. If $\Phi(u) \equiv \phi_0' + \phi_1'u + \phi_2'u^2 + \phi_3'u^3 + \phi_4'u^4$ modulo $P(u)$, then it can be shown that

$$\phi_0' = m_0$$

$$\phi_1' = m_0 + m_1 + m_3 + m_4 + m_5$$

$$\phi_2' = m_2 + m_5 + m_6 \qquad\qquad (4.1)$$

$$\phi_3' = m_0 + m_2 + m_4 + m_5$$

$$\phi_4' = m_0 + m_1 + m_2 + m_3 + m_5 + m_6.$$

Letting $m_7 = z_3 \cdot y_2$, the ordinary polynomial product $\Phi(u) = Z(u)Y(u) = \phi_0 + \phi_1 u + \phi_2 u^2 + \phi_3 u^3 + \phi_4 u^4 + \phi_5 u^5$ can be computed from (4.1) and the various coefficients ϕ_i, $i = 0, 1, \ldots, 5$ are given by,

$$\phi_0 = m_0$$

$$\phi_1 = m_0 + m_1 + m_3 + m_4 + m_5 + m_7$$

$$\phi_2 = m_2 + m_5 + m_6 + m_7$$

$$\phi_3 = m_0 + m_2 + m_4 + m_5$$

$$\phi_4 = m_0 + m_1 + m_2 + m_3 + m_5 + m_6 + m_7$$

$$\phi_5 = m_7.$$

Hence the bilinear form for the computation of the above periodic convolution is given by,

$$
\begin{bmatrix} \phi_0 \\ \phi_1 \\ \phi_2 \\ \phi_3 \\ \phi_4 \\ \phi_5 \end{bmatrix} =
\begin{bmatrix}
1 & 0 & 0 & 0 & 0 & 0 & 0 & 0 \\
1 & 1 & 0 & 1 & 1 & 1 & 0 & 1 \\
0 & 0 & 1 & 0 & 0 & 1 & 1 & 1 \\
1 & 0 & 1 & 0 & 1 & 1 & 0 & 0 \\
1 & 1 & 1 & 1 & 0 & 1 & 1 & 1 \\
0 & 0 & 0 & 0 & 0 & 0 & 0 & 1
\end{bmatrix}
\begin{bmatrix}
\begin{bmatrix}
1 & 0 & 0 & 0 \\
1 & 0 & 1 & 0 \\
1 & 1 & 1 & 1 \\
0 & 1 & 0 & 1 \\
1 & 0 & 1 & 1 \\
1 & 1 & 0 & 1 \\
0 & 1 & 1 & 0 \\
0 & 0 & 0 & 1
\end{bmatrix}
\begin{bmatrix} z_0 \\ z_1 \\ z_2 \\ z_3 \end{bmatrix}
\times
\begin{bmatrix}
1 & 0 & 0 \\
1 & 0 & 1 \\
1 & 1 & 1 \\
0 & 1 & 0 \\
1 & 0 & 1 \\
1 & 1 & 0 \\
0 & 1 & 1 \\
0 & 0 & 1
\end{bmatrix}
\begin{bmatrix} y_0 \\ y_1 \\ y_2 \end{bmatrix}
\end{bmatrix}
$$

$$= P[Q\underline{z} \times R\underline{y}].$$

The generator matrix for the corresponding (8,4,3) single error correcting code is,

$$C = \begin{bmatrix} 1 & 1 & 1 & 0 & 1 & 1 & 0 & 0 \\ 0 & 0 & 1 & 1 & 0 & 1 & 1 & 0 \\ 0 & 1 & 1 & 0 & 1 & 0 & 1 & 0 \\ 0 & 0 & 1 & 1 & 1 & 1 & 0 & 1 \end{bmatrix}$$

This is the best possible binary code in terms of its rate and distance properties, i.e., it is not possible to find a code with the same n and d for which k is larger.

4.1.2 Bilinear convolution algorithm of length 16 and the corresponding codes

Since $N = k+d-1 = 16$, we have $k+d = 17$. Let $k = 8$ and $d = 9$; therefore,

$$Z(u) = z_0 + z_1 u + z_2 u^2 + z_3 u^3 + z_4 u^4 + z_5 u^5 + z_6 u^6 + z_7 u^7$$

and,

$$Y(u) = y_0 + y_1 u + y_2 u^2 + y_3 u^3 + y_4 u^4 + y_5 u^5 + y_6 u^6 + y_7 u^7 + y_8 u^8 .$$

Choosing $P(u) = u^3 (u^2+1)(u^3+u+1)(u^3+u^2+1)(u^2+u+1)$ and $s = 3$, it can be shown that the polynomial product $\Phi(u) = Z(u)Y(u)$ can be computed using the algorithm $P[Q\underline{z} \times R\underline{y}]$, where the matrices P, Q and R are given by,

$$
P =
\begin{bmatrix}
1 & 0 & 0 & 0 & 0 & 0 & 0 & 0 & 0 & 0 & 0 & 0 & 0 & 0 & 0 & 0 & 0 & 0 & 0 & 0 & 0 & 0 & 0 & 0 & 0 & 0 & 0 & 0 & 0 & 0 & 0 \\
1 & 1 & 0 & 1 & 0 & 0 & 0 & 0 & 0 & 0 & 0 & 0 & 0 & 0 & 0 & 0 & 0 & 0 & 0 & 0 & 0 & 0 & 0 & 0 & 0 & 0 & 0 & 0 & 0 & 0 \\
1 & 1 & 1 & 0 & 1 & 0 & 0 & 0 & 0 & 0 & 0 & 0 & 0 & 0 & 0 & 0 & 0 & 0 & 0 & 0 & 0 & 0 & 0 & 0 & 0 & 0 & 0 & 0 & 0 & 0 \\
1 & 0 & 0 & 0 & 0 & 1 & 1 & 1 & 0 & 1 & 1 & 0 & 0 & 1 & 0 & 1 & 1 & 0 & 1 & 1 & 0 & 0 & 1 & 1 & 0 & 0 & 1 & 1 \\
1 & 1 & 0 & 1 & 0 & 1 & 1 & 0 & 1 & 0 & 1 & 1 & 0 & 0 & 1 & 1 & 0 & 0 & 0 & 1 & 1 & 1 & 0 & 1 & 1 & 1 & 0 & 0 \\
1 & 1 & 1 & 0 & 1 & 1 & 1 & 1 & 1 & 0 & 1 & 1 & 0 & 0 & 0 & 1 & 0 & 0 & 0 & 1 & 0 & 1 & 1 & 0 & 0 & 0 & 0 \\
0 & 0 & 0 & 0 & 0 & 0 & 1 & 0 & 0 & 0 & 1 & 1 & 0 & 0 & 0 & 1 & 0 & 0 & 1 & 1 & 1 & 0 & 1 & 0 & 0 & 1 & 1 \\
1 & 0 & 0 & 0 & 0 & 0 & 0 & 1 & 0 & 0 & 0 & 1 & 1 & 1 & 0 & 1 & 0 & 1 & 0 & 0 & 1 & 0 & 1 & 1 & 1 & 1 & 0 & 0 \\
1 & 1 & 0 & 1 & 0 & 0 & 0 & 1 & 0 & 0 & 0 & 0 & 1 & 1 & 1 & 0 & 0 & 0 & 1 & 0 & 1 & 1 & 1 & 1 & 0 & 0 & 0 & 0 \\
1 & 1 & 1 & 0 & 1 & 0 & 0 & 1 & 0 & 0 & 0 & 1 & 0 & 1 & 1 & 0 & 1 & 1 & 0 & 1 & 0 & 1 & 1 & 0 & 0 & 0 & 0 & 0 \\
1 & 0 & 0 & 0 & 0 & 1 & 1 & 0 & 0 & 1 & 1 & 0 & 1 & 1 & 1 & 0 & 0 & 1 & 0 & 1 & 0 & 1 & 1 & 1 & 0 & 0 & 1 & 1 \\
1 & 1 & 0 & 1 & 0 & 1 & 1 & 1 & 1 & 1 & 0 & 1 & 0 & 1 & 1 & 0 & 1 & 0 & 0 & 0 & 0 & 0 & 0 & 1 & 1 & 1 & 0 & 0 \\
1 & 1 & 0 & 1 & 0 & 1 & 1 & 1 & 1 & 0 & 1 & 1 & 0 & 1 & 1 & 0 & 1 & 1 & 1 & 0 & 0 & 1 & 0 & 1 & 0 & 0 & 0 & 0 \\
0 & 0 & 0 & 0 & 0 & 0 & 0 & 0 & 0 & 0 & 0 & 0 & 0 & 0 & 0 & 0 & 0 & 0 & 0 & 0 & 0 & 0 & 0 & 0 & 1 & 0 & 0 & 1 & 1 \\
0 & 0 & 0 & 0 & 0 & 0 & 0 & 0 & 0 & 0 & 0 & 0 & 0 & 0 & 0 & 0 & 0 & 0 & 0 & 0 & 0 & 0 & 0 & 0 & 1 & 1 & 1 & 0 & 0 \\
0 & 0 & 0 & 0 & 0 & 0 & 0 & 0 & 0 & 0 & 0 & 0 & 0 & 0 & 0 & 0 & 0 & 0 & 0 & 0 & 0 & 0 & 0 & 0 & 1 & 0 & 0 & 0 & 0
\end{bmatrix}
$$

$$Q^T = \begin{bmatrix} 1 & 0 & 0 & 1 & 1 & 1 & 0 & 1 & 1 & 0 & 1 & 1 & 0 & 0 & 1 & 0 & 1 & 1 & 0 & 0 & 1 & 0 & 1 & 0 & 0 & 0 & 0 & 0 \\ 0 & 1 & 0 & 1 & 0 & 0 & 1 & 1 & 0 & 1 & 1 & 0 & 1 & 0 & 1 & 1 & 0 & 0 & 1 & 0 & 1 & 1 & 0 & 0 & 0 & 0 & 0 & 0 \\ 0 & 0 & 1 & 0 & 1 & 1 & 0 & 1 & 1 & 1 & 0 & 0 & 0 & 1 & 0 & 1 & 1 & 0 & 0 & 1 & 0 & 1 & 1 & 0 & 0 & 0 & 0 & 0 \\ 0 & 0 & 0 & 0 & 0 & 0 & 1 & 1 & 1 & 0 & 1 & 1 & 1 & 0 & 0 & 1 & 1 & 1 & 0 & 1 & 1 & 1 & 0 & 0 & 0 & 0 & 0 & 0 \\ 0 & 0 & 0 & 0 & 0 & 1 & 0 & 1 & 0 & 1 & 1 & 0 & 1 & 1 & 1 & 0 & 1 & 1 & 1 & 1 & 0 & 0 & 0 & 0 & 0 & 0 & 0 & 0 \\ 0 & 0 & 0 & 0 & 0 & 0 & 1 & 1 & 1 & 1 & 0 & 1 & 1 & 1 & 0 & 0 & 0 & 1 & 1 & 0 & 0 & 1 & 1 & 0 & 0 & 0 & 1 & 1 \\ 0 & 0 & 0 & 0 & 0 & 1 & 0 & 1 & 1 & 0 & 1 & 1 & 0 & 1 & 1 & 1 & 0 & 0 & 1 & 1 & 1 & 0 & 1 & 0 & 1 & 1 & 0 & 0 \\ 0 & 0 & 0 & 0 & 0 & 0 & 1 & 1 & 0 & 1 & 1 & 1 & 0 & 0 & 1 & 0 & 1 & 1 & 0 & 0 & 1 & 0 & 1 & 1 & 1 & 0 & 1 & 0 \end{bmatrix}$$

and,

$$R^T = \begin{bmatrix} 1 & 0 & 0 & 1 & 1 & 1 & 0 & 1 & 1 & 0 & 1 & 1 & 0 & 0 & 1 & 0 & 1 & 1 & 0 & 0 & 1 & 0 & 1 & 0 & 0 & 0 & 0 & 0 \\ 0 & 1 & 0 & 1 & 0 & 0 & 1 & 1 & 0 & 1 & 1 & 0 & 1 & 0 & 1 & 1 & 0 & 0 & 1 & 0 & 1 & 1 & 0 & 0 & 0 & 0 & 0 & 0 \\ 0 & 0 & 1 & 0 & 1 & 1 & 0 & 1 & 1 & 1 & 0 & 0 & 0 & 1 & 0 & 1 & 1 & 0 & 0 & 1 & 0 & 1 & 1 & 0 & 0 & 0 & 0 & 0 \\ 0 & 0 & 0 & 0 & 0 & 0 & 1 & 1 & 1 & 0 & 1 & 1 & 1 & 0 & 0 & 1 & 1 & 1 & 0 & 1 & 1 & 1 & 0 & 0 & 0 & 0 & 0 & 0 \\ 0 & 0 & 0 & 0 & 0 & 1 & 0 & 1 & 0 & 1 & 1 & 0 & 1 & 1 & 1 & 0 & 1 & 1 & 1 & 1 & 0 & 0 & 0 & 0 & 0 & 0 & 0 & 0 \\ 0 & 0 & 0 & 0 & 0 & 0 & 1 & 1 & 1 & 1 & 0 & 1 & 1 & 1 & 0 & 0 & 0 & 1 & 1 & 0 & 0 & 1 & 1 & 0 & 0 & 0 & 0 & 0 \\ 0 & 0 & 0 & 0 & 0 & 1 & 0 & 1 & 1 & 0 & 1 & 1 & 0 & 1 & 1 & 1 & 0 & 0 & 1 & 1 & 1 & 0 & 1 & 0 & 0 & 0 & 1 & 1 \\ 0 & 0 & 0 & 0 & 0 & 0 & 1 & 1 & 0 & 1 & 1 & 1 & 0 & 0 & 1 & 0 & 1 & 1 & 0 & 0 & 1 & 0 & 1 & 0 & 1 & 1 & 0 & 0 \\ 0 & 0 & 0 & 0 & 0 & 1 & 0 & 1 & 1 & 1 & 0 & 0 & 1 & 0 & 1 & 1 & 0 & 0 & 1 & 0 & 1 & 1 & 0 & 1 & 1 & 0 & 1 & 0 \end{bmatrix}$$

The matrix Q^T is also the generator matrix of a $(28,8,9)$ four error-correcting code. The above matrices can be easily modified to accomodate the case when $k = 6$ and $d = 11$. The generator matrix of the corresponding $(28,6,11)$ five error-correcting code can be shown to be,

$$
C = \begin{bmatrix}
1 & 0 & 0 & 1 & 1 & 1 & 0 & 1 & 1 & 0 & 1 & 1 & 0 & 0 & 1 & 0 & 1 & 1 & 0 & 0 & 1 & 0 & 1 & 0 & 0 & 0 & 0 & 0 \\
0 & 1 & 0 & 1 & 0 & 0 & 1 & 1 & 0 & 1 & 1 & 0 & 1 & 0 & 1 & 1 & 0 & 0 & 1 & 0 & 1 & 1 & 0 & 0 & 0 & 0 & 0 & 0 \\
0 & 0 & 1 & 0 & 1 & 1 & 0 & 1 & 1 & 1 & 0 & 0 & 0 & 1 & 0 & 1 & 1 & 0 & 0 & 1 & 0 & 1 & 1 & 0 & 0 & 0 & 0 & 0 \\
0 & 0 & 0 & 0 & 0 & 0 & 1 & 1 & 1 & 0 & 1 & 1 & 1 & 0 & 0 & 1 & 1 & 1 & 0 & 1 & 1 & 1 & 0 & 0 & 0 & 0 & 1 & 1 \\
0 & 0 & 0 & 0 & 0 & 1 & 0 & 1 & 0 & 1 & 1 & 0 & 1 & 0 & 1 & 0 & 1 & 1 & 1 & 1 & 0 & 0 & 0 & 0 & 1 & 1 & 0 & 0 \\
0 & 0 & 0 & 0 & 0 & 0 & 1 & 1 & 1 & 1 & 0 & 1 & 1 & 1 & 0 & 0 & 0 & 1 & 1 & 0 & 0 & 1 & 1 & 1 & 1 & 0 & 1 & 0 \\
\end{bmatrix}
$$

Similarly, the generator matrix of the (28,10,7) three error-correcting code can be obtained as,

$$
C = \begin{bmatrix}
1 & 0 & 0 & 1 & 1 & 1 & 0 & 1 & 1 & 0 & 1 & 1 & 0 & 0 & 1 & 0 & 1 & 1 & 0 & 0 & 1 & 0 & 1 & 0 & 0 & 0 & 0 & 0 \\
0 & 1 & 0 & 1 & 0 & 0 & 1 & 1 & 0 & 1 & 1 & 0 & 1 & 0 & 1 & 1 & 0 & 0 & 1 & 0 & 1 & 1 & 0 & 0 & 0 & 0 & 0 & 0 \\
0 & 0 & 1 & 0 & 1 & 1 & 0 & 1 & 1 & 1 & 0 & 0 & 0 & 1 & 0 & 1 & 1 & 0 & 0 & 1 & 0 & 1 & 1 & 0 & 0 & 0 & 0 & 0 \\
0 & 0 & 0 & 0 & 0 & 0 & 1 & 1 & 1 & 0 & 1 & 1 & 1 & 0 & 0 & 1 & 1 & 1 & 0 & 1 & 1 & 1 & 0 & 0 & 0 & 0 & 0 & 0 \\
0 & 0 & 0 & 0 & 0 & 1 & 0 & 1 & 0 & 1 & 1 & 0 & 1 & 1 & 1 & 0 & 1 & 1 & 1 & 1 & 0 & 0 & 0 & 0 & 0 & 0 & 0 & 0 \\
0 & 0 & 0 & 0 & 0 & 0 & 1 & 1 & 1 & 1 & 0 & 1 & 1 & 1 & 0 & 0 & 0 & 1 & 1 & 0 & 0 & 1 & 1 & 0 & 0 & 0 & 0 & 0 \\
0 & 0 & 0 & 0 & 0 & 1 & 0 & 1 & 1 & 0 & 1 & 1 & 0 & 1 & 1 & 1 & 0 & 0 & 1 & 1 & 1 & 0 & 1 & 0 & 0 & 0 & 0 & 0 \\
0 & 0 & 0 & 0 & 0 & 0 & 1 & 1 & 0 & 1 & 1 & 1 & 0 & 0 & 1 & 0 & 1 & 1 & 0 & 0 & 1 & 0 & 1 & 0 & 0 & 0 & 1 & 1 \\
0 & 0 & 0 & 0 & 0 & 1 & 0 & 1 & 1 & 1 & 0 & 0 & 1 & 0 & 1 & 1 & 0 & 0 & 1 & 0 & 1 & 1 & 0 & 0 & 1 & 1 & 0 & 0 \\
0 & 0 & 0 & 0 & 0 & 0 & 1 & 1 & 1 & 0 & 1 & 0 & 0 & 1 & 0 & 1 & 1 & 0 & 0 & 1 & 0 & 1 & 1 & 1 & 1 & 0 & 1 & 0 \\
\end{bmatrix}
$$

Table 4.1 lists selected binary linear codes that can be obtained using the CRT based convolution algorithm for length up to 30 along with their parameters.

TABLE 4.1
BINARY LINEAR CODES OBTAINED FROM THE APERIODIC
CONVOLUTION ALGORITHM

Length of Conv. N	Codelength n	Dimension k	Design Distance d
5	6*	3	3
6	8*	4	3
	8	2	5
7	10	5	3
	10*	3	5
8	12	6	3
	12*	4	5
	12*	2	7
9	14	7	3
	14*	5	5
	14*	3	7
10	16	8	3
	16	6	5
	16*	4	7
11	18	9	3
	18	7	5
	18*	5	7
	18*	3	9
12	20	10	3
	20	8	5
	20	6	7
	20*	4	9

37

TABLE 4.1 (CONTINUED)

Length of Conv. N	Codelength n	Dimension k	Design Distance d
13	22	9	5
	22	7	7
	22*	5	9
	22*	3	11
14	24	10	5
	24	8	7
	24*	6	9
	24*	4	11
15	26	11	5
	26	9	7
	26*	7	9
	26*	5	11
	26*	3	13
16	28	10	7
	28*	8	9
	28*	6	11
	28*	4	13
17	30	11	7
	30	9	9
	30*	7	11
	30*	5	13
	30	3	15

Note that all the codes marked with an asterisk are either the same as the best known codes or very close to the already known best codes

[10,20]. The list of binary codes that can be derived using the algorithm in this section is quite large and we have derived codes of length up to 100 and distance up to 41. There are certain advantages to this approach for linear code generation, some of which have not been previously observed:

(i)   Knowing k and d, we can derive an error-correcting code for these parameters. A wide choice is possible because the codes are not restricted to be cyclic.

(ii)   The codes have the unique property that k+d-1 = constant; this gives a particular set of codes of length n. For example, the (26,9,7), (26,7,9), and (26,5,11) codes belong to the same set. There is, therefore, a systematic way to decrease (increase) k in order to increase (decrease) d for a given n.

(iii)   The columns of the generator matrix C correspond to (a) multiplications required to compute the product $Z(u)Y(u)$ modulo $P(u)$ or, (b) multiplications required to compute the product $\bar{Z}(u)\bar{Y}(u)$ modulo u^s (wraparound). We can decrease k by suitably shortening the columns of the matrix C. The columns corresponding to (a) are shortened from the bottom and the columns corresponding to (b) are shortened from the top. For example, the generator matrix of the (12,6,3) code is given by,

$$C = \begin{bmatrix} 1 & 0 & 1 & 1 & 0 & 1 & 1 & 0 & 1 & 0 & 0 & 0 \\ 0 & 1 & 1 & 0 & 1 & 1 & 0 & 1 & 1 & 0 & 0 & 0 \\ 0 & 0 & 0 & 1 & 0 & 1 & 1 & 1 & 0 & 0 & 0 & 0 \\ 0 & 0 & 0 & 0 & 1 & 1 & 1 & 0 & 1 & 0 & 0 & 0 \\ 0 & 0 & 0 & 1 & 0 & 1 & 0 & 1 & 1 & 0 & 1 & 1 \\ 0 & 0 & 0 & 0 & 1 & 1 & 1 & 1 & 0 & 1 & 0 & 1 \end{bmatrix} \qquad (4.2)$$

Here, the last 3 columns of the matrix C corresponds to the wraparound. Hence, the generator matrix of the (12,4,5) code can be obtained by shortening the columns of the matrix C appropriately as shown in (4.2). The generator matrix of the (12,4,5) code, therefore, is

$$C = \begin{bmatrix} 1 & 0 & 1 & 1 & 0 & 1 & 1 & 0 & 1 & 0 & 0 & 0 \\ 0 & 1 & 1 & 0 & 1 & 1 & 0 & 1 & 1 & 0 & 0 & 0 \\ 0 & 0 & 0 & 1 & 0 & 1 & 1 & 1 & 0 & 0 & 1 & 1 \\ 0 & 0 & 0 & 0 & 1 & 1 & 1 & 0 & 1 & 1 & 0 & 1 \end{bmatrix} \qquad (4.3)$$

Thus, a change in k does not imply a significant change in the encoding procedure. It is worthwhile to mention here that a change in k does not alter the decoding procedure significantly. This point is illustrated further by the generalised decoding procedure presented in the next chapter.

(iv) For a given value of k, it is possible to decrease (increase) the minimum distance d of the code by simply deleting (adding) columns of the generator matrix, thereby leading to an appropriate decrease (increase) in the length n of the code. The encoder/decoder design for all such

40

codes remains **essentially unaltered**. The system designer, therefore, can incorporate a wide range of different codes in a single encoder/decoder structure. This property is established in Chapter 5.

(v) The above two points indicate that the error-correcting capability $\lfloor (d-1)/2 \rfloor$, of the codes generated can be altered quite easily, a feature which can be valuable in a fluctuating noise environment. Now, in many cases, one has to change code families and, consequently, the entire encoding/decoding procedure to accommodate such situations.

4.2 CRT-Based Convolution Algorithm Over GF(3) and Related Codes

Given below is a list of certain polynomials over GF(3) of degree less than 4,

degree 1: u, $u+1$, $u+2$

degree 2: u^2, u^2+1, u^2+u+1, u^2+u+2, u^2+2u+2, u^2+2u+1

degree 3: u^3, u^3+1, u^3+2, u^3+2u+1, u^3+2u+2, u^3+u^2+2,

u^3+u^2+u+2, u^3+u^2+2u+1, u^3+2u^2+1, u^3+2u^2+u+1,

u^3+2u^2+2u+2

Once again, for each degree i, only those polynomials are listed which are not products of two distinct polynomials of lower degree. Based on the above polynomials, given below is the list of polynomials of degrees upto 10, obtained so as to minimise the complexity of computing the polynomial product $Z(u)Y(u)$ modulo $P(u)$,

D = 3: $P(u) = u(u+1)(u+2)$

D = 4: $P(u) = (u+1)(u+2)(u^2+u+2)$

D = 5: $P(u) = u(u+1)(u+2)(u^2+u+2)$

$D = 6$: $P(u) = u^2(u+1)(u+2)(u^2+u+2)$

$D = 7$: $P(u) = u(u+1)(u+2)(u^2+u+2)(u^2+2u+2)$

$D = 8$: $P(u) = u(u+1)(u^2+1)(u^2+u+2)(u^2+2u+1)$

$D = 9$: $P(u) = u(u+1)(u+2)(u^2+1)(u^2+u+2)(u^2+2u+2)$

$D =10$: $P(u) = u^2(u+1)(u+2)(u^2+1)(u^2+u+2)(u^2+2u+2)$

In the following, we derive bilinear convolution algorithm of length 8 and the corresponding code over GF(3).

4.2.1 <u>Bilinear convolution algorithm of length 8 and the corresponding</u>

<u>code</u>

Since $N = k+d-1 = 8$, we have $k+d = 9$.   Let $k = 4$ and $d = 5$. Therefore, $Z(u) = z_0+z_1u+...+z_3u^3$ and $Y(u) = y_0+y_1u+...+y_4u^4$.   We choose $P(u) = u(u+1)(u+2)(u^2+u+2)(u^2+2u+2)$ and $s = 1$ to compute the aperiodic convolution $\Phi(u) = Z(u)Y(u)$.   Let $P_1(u) = u$, $P_2(u) = (u+1)$, $P_3(u) = (u+2)$, $P_4(u) = (u^2+u+2)$, and $P_5(u) = (u^2+2u+2)$.   Reducing the polynomials $Z(u)$ and $Y(u)$ modulo each of $P_i(u)$, we obtain

$$Z_1(u) \equiv Z(u) \quad \text{modulo } u$$

$$= z_0$$

$$Y_1(u) \equiv Y(u) \quad \text{modulo } u$$

$$= y_0.$$

Let $m_0 = z_0 \cdot y_0$.   Similarly,

$$Z_2(u) \equiv Z(u) \quad \text{modulo } (u+1)$$

$$= z_0+2z_1+z_2+2z_3$$

$$Y_2(u) \equiv Y(u) \quad \text{modulo } (u+1)$$

$$= y_0+2y_1+y_2+2y_3+y_4$$

Let

$$m_1 = (z_0+2z_1+z_2+2z_3) \cdot (y_0+2y_1+y_2+2y_3+y_4).$$

Also, $\qquad Z_3(u) \equiv Z(u) \quad \text{modulo } (u+2)$

$$= z_0 + z_1 + z_2 + z_3$$

$$Y_3(u) \equiv Y(u) \quad \text{modulo } (u+2)$$

$$= y_0 + y_1 + y_2 + y_3 + y_4.$$

Let, $\qquad m_2 = (z_0 + z_1 + z_2 + z_3) \cdot (y_0 + y_1 + y_2 + y_3 + y_4).$

Also, $\qquad Z_4(u) \equiv Z(u) \quad \text{modulo } (u^2 + u + 2)$

$$= (z_0 + z_2 + 2z_3) + (z_1 + 2z_2 + 2z_3)u$$

$$Y_4(u) \equiv Y(u) \quad \text{modulo } (u^2 + u + 2)$$

$$= (y_0 + y_2 + 2y_3 + 2y_4) + (y_1 + 2y_2 + 2y_3)u.$$

Let, $\qquad m_3 = (z_0 + z_2 + 2z_3) \cdot (y_0 + y_2 + 2y_3 + 2y_4)$

$$m_4 = (z_1 + 2z_2 + 2z_3) \cdot (y_1 + 2y_2 + 2y_3)$$

$$m_5 = (z_0 + z_1 + z_3) \cdot (y_0 + y_1 + y_3 + 2y_4).$$

Also, $\qquad Z_5(u) \equiv Z(u) \quad \text{modulo } (u^2 + 2u + 2)$

$$= (z_0 + z_2 + z_3) + (z_1 + z_2 + 2z_3)u$$

$$Y_5(u) \equiv Y(u) \quad \text{modulo } (u^2 + 2u + 2)$$

$$= (y_0 + y_2 + y_3 + 2y_4) + (y_1 + y_2 + 2y_3)u.$$

Let, $\qquad m_6 = (z_0 + z_2 + z_3) \cdot (y_0 + y_2 + y_3 + 2y_4)$

$$m_7 = (z_1 + z_2 + 2z_3) \cdot (y_1 + y_2 + 2y_3)$$

$$m_8 = (z_0 + z_1 + 2z_2) \cdot (y_0 + y_1 + 2y_2 + 2y_4).$$

Let $m_9 = z_3 \cdot y_4$ (wraparound). The multiplications m_0, $m_1, \ldots,$ m_8 are sufficient to compute $\Phi(u) \equiv Z(u)Y(u)$ modulo $P(u)$.

The generator matrix of the associated $(10,4,5)$ linear code defined over $GF(3)$ is given by,

$$C = \begin{bmatrix} 1 & 1 & 1 & 1 & 0 & 1 & 1 & 0 & 1 & 0 \\ 0 & 2 & 1 & 0 & 1 & 1 & 0 & 1 & 1 & 0 \\ 0 & 1 & 1 & 1 & 2 & 0 & 1 & 1 & 2 & 0 \\ 0 & 2 & 1 & 2 & 2 & 1 & 1 & 2 & 0 & 0 \\ 0 & 1 & 1 & 2 & 0 & 2 & 2 & 0 & 2 & 1 \end{bmatrix}$$

The above code compares well with the only known nontrivial perfect nonbinary (11,6,5) ternary code [9]. Also, it can be easily observed that the length of ternary codes is smaller than the length of binary codes for the same value of k and d. This is due to the fact that as the field of constants grows in size, the number of polynomials of any degree defined over the field also grows. Table 4.2 contains a list of selected ternary codes that can be obtained from the CRT-based aperiodic convolution algorithms.

TABLE 4.2

TERNARY LINEAR CODES OBTAINED FROM THE APERIODIC

CONVOLUTION ALGORITHM

Length of Conv. N	Codelength n	Dimension k	Design Distance d
5	6	3	3
6	7	4	3
	7	2	5
7	9	5	3
	9	3	5
8	10	6	3
	10	4	5
	10	2	7
9	12	7	3
	12	5	5
	12	3	7
10	13	8	3
	13	6	5
	13	4	7
11	15	9	3
	15	7	5
	15	5	7
	15	3	9
12	17	10	3
	17	8	5
	17	6	7
	17	4	9

4.3 A Shift-Register Based Encoding Procedure

Let $P(u)$ be of the form $P(u) = \prod_{i=1}^{t} P_i(u)$ and $Z(u)$ represent the k-dimensional information vector as a polynomial of degree k-1. The encoding procedure then corresponds to the following steps:

(i) Compute $Z_i(u) \equiv Z(u)$ modulo $P_i(u)$, $i = 1,2,\ldots,t$.

(ii) Form the appropriate linear combinations of the coefficients of $Z_i(u)$, so that the product $Z_i(u)Y_i(u)$ modulo $P_i(u)$ can be computed.

(iii) Form the appropriate linear combinations of the coefficients of $\bar{Z}(u)$, so that the product $\bar{Z}(u)\bar{Y}(u)$ modulo u^s can be computed (wraparound).

Note that step (iii) can be treated as a special case of step (ii) and, therefore, we will only study (i) and (ii) for the encoder design. It is clear that $Z_i(u)$ is the remainder obtained by dividing $Z(u)$ by $P_i(u)$. Such a procedure can be implemented by a division circuit, which is a α_i-stage shift-register with feedback connections determined according to $P_i(u)$ ($\alpha_i = \deg[P(u)]$) [9]. Figure 4.1 shows the three basic types of units that constitute a shift-register. Based on Figure 4.1, the general configuration of a shift-register based division circuit is shown in Figure 4.2.

The multipliers and the adders shown in Figure 4.2 are from the appropriate field. In the binary case, the multipliers and the adders are from GF(2) and, consequently, each of the multiplier coefficient is either 0 (open circuit) or 1 (short circuit) and the adders are replaced by exclusive-OR gates. We require t such circuits, one for each of the polynomials $P_i(u)$. Figure 4.3(a)-(f) shows the shift-register

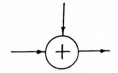

(a). Adder

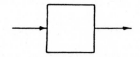

(b). Delay or storage unit

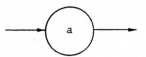

(c). Multiplier (multiplies by a)

Figure 4.1. The three basic units for shift-register
implementation

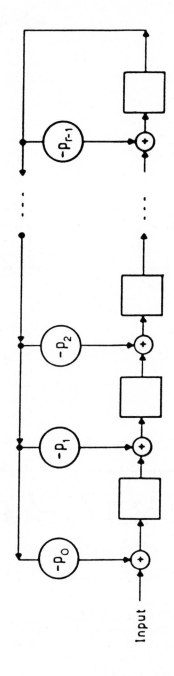

Figure 4.2. A shift-register circuit for division by a polynomial

$$P(u) = u^r + p_{r-1}u^{r-1} + \ldots + p_1 u + p_0$$

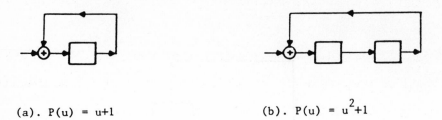

(a). P(u) = u+1

(b). P(u) = u^2+1

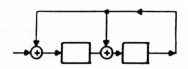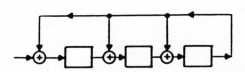

(c). P(u) = u^2+u+1

(d). P(u) = u^3+u^2+u+1

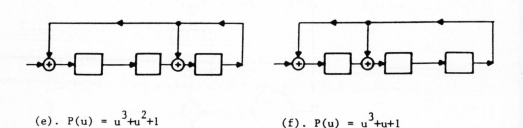

(e). P(u) = u^3+u^2+1

(f). P(u) = u^3+u+1

Figure 4.3. Examples of shift-register circuit for division
by a polynomial P(u)

configurations with feedback connections for some of the polynomials defined over GF(2).

If $P_i(u)$ is irreducible over the field of computation, $Z_i(u)Y_i(u)$ modulo $P_i(u)$ is computed by first computing $Z_i(u)Y_i(u)$ and then reducing the product modulo $P_i(u)$. Therefore, in this case, the equations for the linear combinations of the coefficients of $Z_i(u)$ are independent of $P_i(u)$. Figure 4.4 shows the linear combinations of the coefficients of $Z_i(u)$ as required by (ii) for some of the polynomials $P_i(u)$ defined over GF(2).

We now consider the encoder design for the (24,6,9) binary code. Here, $P(u) = u^2(u^2+1)(u^2+u+1)(u^3+u^2+1)(u^3+u+1)$ and $s = 2$. The shift-register implementation of the encoder is shown in Figure 4.5. The information vector is represented as $Z(u) = z_0+z_1u+...+z_5u^5$. The encoder circuit requires 14 delay units and 17 exclusive-OR gates.

4.4   Multidimensional Convolution Algorithm And Related Codes

It was demonstrated in Section 3.3 that a one-dimensional polynomial product can be converted into a multidimensional polynomial product for composite k and d, where k and d are the lengths of the polynomials $Z(u)$ and $Y(u)$, respectively. For example, if $k = k_1c$ and $d = d_1c$, the product $Z(u)Y(u)$ is computed as a two-dimensional polynomial product. The first dimension corresponds to the product of two polynomials of degrees $(c-1)$ each and the second dimension corresponds to the product of two polynomials of degrees (k_1-1) and (d_1-1). Each of these products can be computed either by using the algorithms derived on the basis of the CRT or they could be further decomposed into multidimensional polynomial products.

50

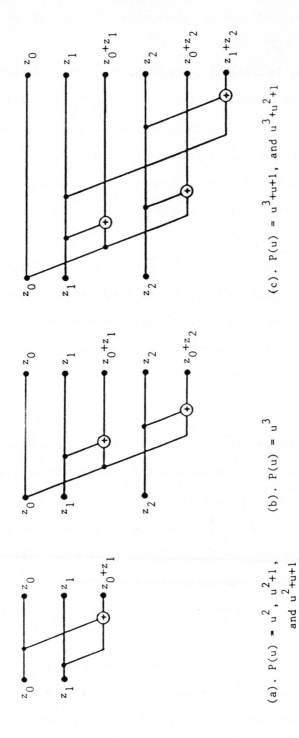

(a). $P(u) = u^2$, u^2+1,
and u^2+u+1

(b). $P(u) = u^3$

(c). $P(u) = u^3+u+1$, and u^3+u^2+1

Figure 4.4. Linear combinations of the coefficients of $Z(u)$ required for
the computation $Z(u)Y(u)$ modulo $P(u)$

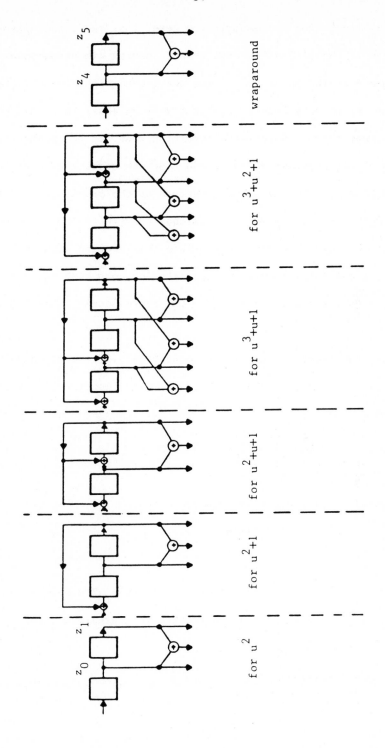

Figure 4.5. A shift-register implementation of the encoder of (24,6,9) binary code

It is clear from the description here, that the first dimension corresponds to the generation of a code V_1 having dimension equal to c and minimum distance equal to c; and the second dimension corresponds to the generation of a code V_2 having dimension equal to k_1 and minimum distance equal to d_1. Hence, the resulting code can be interpreted as the product code obtained as the product of the codes V_1 and V_2 [8]. The properties and the algebraic structure of the product codes are well known, and therefore, the multidimensional convolution approach will not be pursued further. However, we conclude this section with an example illustrating the multidimensional approach for computing the product $\Phi(u) = Z(u)Y(u)$, where k = d = 4, and the corresponding linear code over GF(2).

Using the notations described in Section 3.3, the one-dimensional polynomials Z(u) and Y(u) are converted to two-dimensional polynomials as follows,

$$Z(u,u_1) = (z_0+z_2u_1) + (z_1+z_3u_1)u$$
$$= Z_0(u_1) + Z_1(u_1)u$$

and
$$Y(u,u_1) = (y_0+y_2u_1) + (y_1+y_3u_1)u$$
$$= Y_0(u_1) + Y_1(u_1)u$$

where
$$u_1 = u^2.$$

The two-dimensional product $\Phi(u,u_1) = Z(u,u_1)Y(u,u_1)$ is computed by recursively using Algorithm B described in Appendix A. The computations are given by,

Define
$$\underline{m}_0 = Z_0(u_1) \cdot Y_0(u_1)$$
$$\underline{m}_1 = Z_1(u_1) \cdot Y_1(u_1)$$
$$\underline{m}_2 = [Z_0(u_1)+Z_1(u_1)] \cdot [Y_0(u_1)+Y_1(u_1)].$$

The two-dimensional polynomial $\Phi(u, u_1)$ is then computed as,

$$\Phi(u, u_1) = \underline{m}_0 + (\underline{m}_0 + \underline{m}_1 + \underline{m}_2)u + \underline{m}_1 u^2.$$

$\underline{m}_0$, $\underline{m}_1$ and $\underline{m}_2$, in turn, are computed as follows,

Let,
$$m_0 = z_0 \cdot y_0$$
$$m_1 = z_2 \cdot y_2$$

$$m_2 = (z_0 + z_2) \cdot (y_0 + y_2),$$

then,
$$\underline{m}_0 = m_0 + (m_0 + m_1 + m_2)u_1 + m_1 u_1^2.$$

Let,
$$m_3 = z_1 \cdot y_1$$

$$m_4 = z_3 \cdot y_3$$

$$m_5 = (z_1 + z_3) \cdot (y_1 + y_3)$$

then,
$$\underline{m}_1 = m_3 + (m_3 + m_4 + m_5)u_1 + m_4 u_1^2.$$

Let,
$$m_6 = (z_0 + z_1) \cdot (y_0 + y_1)$$

$$m_7 = (z_2 + z_3) \cdot (y_2 + y_3)$$

$$m_8 = (z_0 + z_1 + z_2 + z_3) \cdot (y_0 + y_1 + y_2 + y_3),$$

then,
$$\underline{m}_2 = m_6 + (m_6 + m_7 + m_8)u_1 + m_7 u_1^2.$$

The polynomial $\Phi(u)$ is obtained from $\Phi(u, u_1)$ by replacing u_1 by u^2. The

resulting $(9,4,4)$ code is the two-dimensional product code, where each

of the constituent codes are $(3,2,2)$ codes. The entire encoding

procedure can be considered as an arrangement of the four information

bits into a square (2×2) matrix with a parity bit adjoined to each row

and column of the matrix. For example, if $z_0 = 1$, $z_1 = 0$, $z_2 = 1$, and $z_3 = 0$,

then the encoding can be shown pictorially as,

1	1	0
0	0	0
1	1	0

It is interesting to observe here that this algorithm is used in the CRT-based convolution approach for the computation $\Phi_i(u) \equiv Z_i(u)Y_i(u)$ modulo $P_i(u)$, if $\deg[P_i(u)] = 4$, and $P_i(u)$ is irreducible.

CHAPTER 5

ERROR-DETECTION AND ERROR-CORRECTION

In this chapter, we consider the problem of error-detection and error-correction for the linear codes generated by the aperiodic convolution algorithms based on the CRT. For a code of length n, obtained as a result of an aperiodic convolution of length N = (k+d-1), it is shown that the decoder design does not change significantly when (i) k and d are varied in a way that N, and consequently, n is a constant, and (ii) k is kept constant and d is varied, changing N and n accordingly. We first consider the problem of error-detection for such codes.

5.1 Error-Detection

With this technique of error control, a received block of digits corresponding to a transmitted codeword is inspected to ascertain if it is a valid codeword. An error pattern will go undetected by the decoder _iff_ it is identical to one of the non-zero codewords. This certainly is the case if the all-zero codeword is transmitted, but also holds for the transmission of an arbitrary codeword due to the linearity of the code.

An (n,k) linear code forms a vector space of dimension k, with corresponding null space of dimension (n-k). The null space is spanned by a set of (n-k) linearly independent (henceforth abbreviated as ℓ.i.) vectors; hence, a received vector is assumed error-free if it satisfies (n-k) ℓ.i. equations. In the following, we establish a procedure to obtain the (n-k) ℓ.i. equations for a given set of codes of length, or complexity, n.

We see from Chapter 3 that the generator matrix C of such a linear code has a block structure. Such a structure arises due to a computation of the type,

$$\Phi_i(u) \equiv Z_i(u)Y_i(u) \text{ modulo } P_i(u) \quad i = 1,2,\dots, t$$

for each of the t relatively prime polynomials $P_i(u)$ of degree α_i, $i = 1,2, \dots, t$. Also, there is a last block that corresponds to the computation $\bar{Z}(u) \; \bar{Y}(u)$ modulo u^s (wraparound). There are $(t+1)$ blocks in the generator matrix C of the (n,k,d) code; we label these blocks of C as C_i, $i = 1,2,\dots, t+1$. The number of columns in each block is given by $M(\alpha_i)$, $i = 1,2,\dots, t+1$. Since _each_ _one_ of the blocks corresponds to a computation of the type described above, it is clear that in each block C_i, there are exactly α_i ($\alpha_{t+1} = s$) columns which are ℓ.i. and the remaining $\left[M(\alpha_i) - \alpha_i\right]$ columns are linearly dependent on them. Therefore, each such block gives rise to $\left[M(\alpha_i) - \alpha_i\right]$ parity check equations. It is assumed that the dimension k of the code under investigation, is greater than α_i, $i = 1,2,\dots, t+1$. This assumption does not restrict our analysis, rather it simplifies it. Any received vector can be segmented into t+1 partitions and the part of the received vector that corresponds to each block C_i should satisfy the $\left[M(\alpha_i) - \alpha_i\right]$ parity check equations for that block. A conventional procedure may be employed to find the $\left[M(\alpha_i) - \alpha_i\right]$ ℓ.i. parity check equations on each block, with the reader referred to [9] for the details. We shall, however, illustrate the technique in the sequel by an example.

Thus, we have established $\left[M(\alpha_i) - \alpha_i\right]$ parity check equations satisfied by the code digits corresponding to each one of the blocks. Moreover, they are also ℓ.i. of the $\left[M(\alpha_j) - \alpha_j\right]$ parity check equations satisfied by the code symbols corresponding to the block C_j, $j \neq i$. The total number of parity check equations obtained by this straightforward procedure is,

$$\sum_{i=1}^{t+1} \left[M(\alpha_i) - \alpha_i\right] = \sum_{i=1}^{t+1} M(\alpha_i) - \sum_{i=1}^{t+1} \alpha_i$$

$$= n - N$$

$$= (n-k) - (d-1)$$

since $N = (k+d-1)$.

This set of $(n-N)$ parity check equations does not change when the value of k is increased (decreased), as n and N are constant for a given set of linear codes obtained from the convolution algorithm for a fixed length. We also observe that there is a need to obtain an additional $(d-1)$ parity check equations which are $\ell.i.$ of those obtained above. These are obtained from the relations **between** the columns of different blocks of C.

Each block C_i, $i = 1,2,\ldots,$ t of C is in two parts. The first α_i columns of each block can always be arranged in a way so as to correspond to the polynomial

$$Z_i(u) \equiv Z(u) \text{ modulo } P_i(u), \quad i = 1,2,\ldots, t.$$

The remaining $\left[M(\alpha_i) - \alpha_i\right]$ columns arise due to the multiplicative complexity of the block C_i, and we have already established the corresponding parity check equations. In each block C_i, let us consider only the first α_i columns. The polynomial $Z(u)$ can be recovered from the residue polynomials $Z_i(u)$, $i = 1,2,\ldots,$ t using the CRT. Such a reconstruction gives a polynomial of degree $D-1$, where D is the degree of the polynomial $P(u)$. However, since the information polynomial is of degree $k-1$, for a reconstructed polynomial to correspond to an information polynomial, its last $\left[(D-1) - (k-1)\right] = (D-k)$ coefficients

should be identically zero. If $Z(u)$ is the reconstructed polynomial,

(i)   The first k coefficients are the information bits, if no errors

have taken place.

(ii)   The expressions for the last $(D-k)$ coefficients provide us with

$(D-k)$ ℓ.i. parity check equations, i.e., if the reconstructed

polynomial $Z(u)$ is,

$$Z(u) = z_0 + z_1 u + \cdots + z_{D-1} u^{D-1}$$

then we have, $z_i \equiv 0 \quad \forall \quad i = k, k+1, \ldots, D-1$ (5.1)

The first α_{t+1} ($= s$) columns of the block corresponding to the

wraparound provide us with the polynomial

$$\bar{Z}(u) = \bar{z}_{k-1} + \bar{z}_{k-2} u + \cdots + \bar{z}_{k-s} u^{s-1}$$ (5.2)

If no errors have taken place, then the corresponding coefficients of

the polynomial $Z(u)$ and $\bar{Z}(u)$ should be the same, i.e.,

$$z_i = \bar{z}_i \qquad i = k-1, \ldots, k-s$$ (5.3)

Equation (5.3) is an additional set of s ℓ.i. equations. The total

number of equations given by (5.1) and (5.3) is $(D-k) + s = (D+s-k)$.

Also, $N = (D+s) = (k+d-1)$ and, therefore, $(D+s-k) = (d-1)$. Hence, the

parity check equations given by (5.1) and (5.3) provide the remaining

$(d-1)$ parity check equations. These equations are also ℓ.i., due to the

fact that any coefficient of a polynomial cannot be expressed as a

linear sum of the other coefficients.

Of these $(d-1)$ parity check equations obtained from (5.1) and

(5.3), the parity check equations given by (5.3) are altered, and

$d_2 = |d_1 - d|$ equations are added to (5.1) or dropped from (5.1) when a new code is selected from the same set, depending on whether k is decreased or increased, where d_1 is the minimum distance of the selected code. Note that all the codes in a given set have the same code length n. It is also worthwhile to mention that the above procedure not only gives the required set of parity check equations, but it also provides the equations that can be used to find the transmitted message polynomial once the received code vector is found to contain no errors. The complete procedure to find the parity check equations is illustrated below for the (12,4,5) code.

Example. Consider the (12,4,5) code. Since $N = k+d-1 = 8$, we have $k+d = 9$. The polynomials are $Z(u) = z_0 + z_1 u + z_2 u^2 + z_3 u^3$ and $Y(u) = y_0 + y_1 u + \cdots + y_4 u^4$. Let $P_1(u) = u^2$, $P_2(u) = (u^2+1)$, and $P_3(u) = (u^2+u+1)$, and therefore, $P(u) = u^2(u^2+1)(u^2+u+1)$ and $s = 2$ are used to compute the aperiodic convolution $\Phi(u) = Z(u)Y(u)$. Reducing the polynomials $Z(u)$ and $Y(u)$ modulo each of $P_i(u)$, we obtain

$$Z_1(u) \equiv Z(u) \text{ modulo } u^2$$

$$= z_0 + z_1 u$$

$$Y_1(u) \equiv Y(u) \text{ modulo } u^2$$

$$= y_0 + y_1 u.$$

Let,
$$m_0 = z_0 \cdot y_0$$
$$m_1 = z_1 \cdot y_0$$
$$m_2 = (z_0 + z_1) \cdot (y_0 + y_1).$$

Also,

$$Z_2(u) \equiv Z(u) \text{ modulo } (u^2+1)$$

$$= (z_0+z_2) +(z_1+z_3)u$$

$$Y_2(u) \equiv Y(u) \text{ modulo } (u^2+1)$$

$$= (y_0+y_2+y_4) + (y_1+y_3)u.$$

Let,

$$m_3 = (z_0+z_2) \cdot (y_0+y_2+y_4)$$

$$m_4 = (z_1+z_3) \cdot (y_1+y_3)$$

$$m_5 = (z_0+z_1+z_2+z_3) \cdot (y_0+y_1+\ldots+y_4).$$

Also,

$$Z_3(u) \equiv Z(u) \text{ modulo } (u^2+u+1)$$

$$= (z_0+z_2+z_3) + (z_1+z_2)u$$

$$Y_3(u) \equiv Y(u) \text{ modulo } (u^2+u+1)$$

$$= (y_0+y_2+y_3) + (y_1+y_2+y_4)u.$$

Let,

$$m_6 = (z_0+z_2+z_3) \cdot (y_0+y_2+y_3)$$

$$m_7 = (z_1+z_2) \cdot (y_1+y_2+y_4)$$

$$m_8 = (z_0+z_1+z_3) \cdot (y_0+y_1+y_3+y_4).$$

For the wraparound, let

$$m_9 = z_3 \cdot y_4$$

$$m_{10} = z_2 \cdot y_3$$

$$m_{11} = (z_3+z_2) \cdot (y_4+y_3).$$

It is easy to establish that the 12 multiplications are sufficient to determine the polynomial product $\Phi_i(u) \equiv Z_i(u)Y_i(u)$ modulo $P_i(u)$ as well as to compute the ordinary polynomial product $Z(u)Y(u)$. The generator matrix of the corresponding (12,4,5) code is given by,

$$
C = \begin{bmatrix}
1 & 0 & 1 & 1 & 0 & 1 & 1 & 0 & 1 & 0 & 0 & 0 \\
0 & 1 & 1 & 0 & 1 & 0 & 0 & 1 & 1 & 0 & 0 & 0 \\
0 & 0 & 0 & 1 & 0 & 1 & 1 & 1 & 0 & 0 & 1 & 1 \\
0 & 0 & 0 & 0 & 1 & 1 & 1 & 0 & 1 & 1 & 0 & 1
\end{bmatrix} = [C_1 | C_2 | C_3 | C_4]
$$

$$
\begin{array}{cccc}
\text{For} & \text{For} & \text{For} & \\
P_1(u) & P_2(u) & P_3(u) & \text{wrap.}
\end{array}
$$

It is worthwhile to mention here that the design minimum distance of the above code is 5, while the actual minimum distance is 6. Each of the blocks C_1, C_2, and C_3 corresponding to the computations modulo $P_1(u)$, $P_2(u)$, and $P_3(u)$, respectively, provide $M(2) - 2 = 3 - 2 = 1$ parity check equation. These equations are given by,

For $P_1(u)$ $c_0 + c_1 + c_2 = 0$

For $P_2(u)$ $c_3 + c_4 + c_5 = 0$ (5.4)

For $P_3(u)$ $c_6 + c_7 + c_8 = 0$

where c_i is the ith digit of the code vector $\underline{c} = (c_0 c_1 \cdots c_{11})$. The block C_4 for the wraparound computation provides 1 equation, given by,

$$c_9 + c_{10} + c_{11} = 0 \qquad\qquad (5.5)$$

Now, if we take

$$Z_i(u) \equiv Z(u) \quad \text{modulo } P_i(u), \quad i = 1,2,3,$$

then, using the CRT, the polynomial $Z(u)$ can be written as

$$Z(u) = z_0 + z_1 u + \ldots + z_5 u^5,$$

where $z_0 = c_0$

$z_1 = c_1$

$z_2 = c_0 + c_1 + c_4 + c_6$

$z_3 = c_0 + c_3 + c_4 + c_7$

$z_4 = c_1 + c_3 + c_4 + c_6$

$z_5 = c_0 + c_1 + c_3 + c_7$

If $Z(u)$ corresponds to a message polynomial of degree 3, then,

$$z_4 = z_5 = 0 \qquad\qquad (5.6)$$

Also, the wraparound corresponds to the polynomial coefficient z_2, and z_3, and therefore,

$$z_3 + c_9 = 0 \quad \text{or} \quad c_0 + c_3 + c_4 + c_7 + c_9 = 0$$

$$\text{and} \quad z_2 + c_{10} = 0 \quad \text{or} \quad c_0 + c_1 + c_4 + c_6 + c_{10} = 0 \qquad (5.7)$$

Equations (5.4) and (5.5) along with (5.6) and (5.7) give the complete set of n-k = 12-4 = 8 ℓ.i. parity check equations that a received vector must satisfy before it is declared error-free for the (12,4,5) code.

If we now were to write the parity check equations for the (12,6,3) code, (5.4) and (5.5) remain unchanged. For k = 6, the message polynomial is of degree 5 and, therefore, there is no parity check equation corresponding to (5.6). The parity check equations due to wraparound become $z_5 + c_9 = 0$ and $z_4 + c_{10} = 0$. Thus, only 2 equations are altered when the parity check equations of the (12,6,3) code are obtained from the equations of the (12,4,5) code.

5.2 Error-Correction

We again consider the block structure of the generator matrix. The polynomial P(u) factors into t relatively prime polynomials

$P_i(u)$, $i = 1,2,\ldots,$ t and there are t such blocks in generator matrix of the code, each block corresponding to a computation of the type,

$$\Phi_i(u) \equiv Z_i(u)Y_i(u) \text{ modulo } P_i(u) \qquad i = 1,2,\ldots, t$$

The last block of the generator matrix arises due to the computation of the wraparound coefficients of the ordinary polynomial product $\Phi(u)$. A key property of such a block structure can be described as follows:

Lemma 5.1. If the polynomial $P_i(u)$ is irreducible, then the block C_i corresponding to the computation $\Phi_i(u) \equiv Z_i(u)Y_i(u)$ modulo $P_i(u)$ is a (n_i,α_i,α_i) code, where $n_i = M(\alpha_i)$.

Proof. For all the polynomials $P_i(u)$ that are irreducible, the computation $\Phi_i(u) \equiv Z_i(u)Y_i(u)$ modulo $P_i(u)$ is done in two steps:

(i) Compute $\Phi_i'(u) = Z_i(u)Y_i(u)$

(ii) Reduce $\Phi_i(u) \equiv \Phi_i'(u)$ modulo $P_i(u)$.

Step (i) corresponds to the computation of the ordinary polynomial product; therefore, if the $\deg\left[P_i(u)\right] = \alpha_i$, then such a computation generates a (n_i,α_i,α_i) code, where $n_i = M(\alpha_i)$, the multiplicative complexity associated with the algorithm for step (i). ∎

The only form of polynomials for which the above procedure is not adopted are the polynomials $P_1(u) = u^{\alpha_1}$, $P_2(u) = (u+a_i)^{\alpha_2}$, and the computation of the wraparound coefficients which is given by the computation $\bar{Z}(u)\bar{Y}(u)$ modulo u^s. In our analysis of the decoding procedure, however, we assume that computations of the type $Z_i(u) \, Y_i(u)$ modulo $(u+a_i)^{\alpha_i}$, $a_i \in F$ are also performed using steps (i) and (ii) above. It may be observed that this assumption does not result in a higher complexity algorithm (which also means a code of larger length for the same dimension k and distance d) for values of $\alpha_i \leqslant 2$. For values of $\alpha_i > 2$, the rise in the complexity is very marginal. Also, such a rise in complexity depends on the field of computation. For example, in the binary case, for $\alpha_i = 3$ and 4, the complexity increases by one multiplication only.

Since each block C_i, $i = 1, 2, \ldots$, $t+1$ is a computation of the type given in (i), each block is a $(n_i, \alpha_i, \alpha_i)$ code, $i = 1, 2, \ldots$, $t+1$, where $n_i = M(\alpha_i)$ and $\alpha_{t+1} = s$. We, therefore, start our attempt to decode a received vector by first partitioning the received digits into $t+1$ blocks, and then independently decoding the received digits for each block C_i. If $ZD_i(u)$ represents the decoded vector for the block C_i, then $ZD_i(u)$ is the same as the transmitted residue $Z_i(u)$ for the block C_i, if no more than $\lfloor (\alpha_i - 1)/2 \rfloor$ errors take place in the part of the received vector corresponding to C_i.

$Z_i(u)$ is decoded erroneously only if more than $\lfloor (\alpha_i - 1)/2 \rfloor$ or at least $(\frac{\alpha_i}{2} + 1)$ (for even α_i) or at least $(\frac{\alpha_i - 1}{2} + 1)$ (for odd α_i) errors take place in the block C_i. Note that for even α_i, a decoding failure takes place if block C_i is received with $\alpha_i/2$ errors. If a decoding failure takes place in a block, then such a block can be eliminated from further analysis. Elimination of such a block C_i essentially means that we have to analyse a code of dimension k and of minimum distance $d - \alpha_i$. However, we have also eliminated <u>at least</u> $\lfloor (\alpha_i - 1)/2 \rfloor + 1$ errors by excluding such a block. Therefore, if we recover $Z(u)$ from the reduced code (code obtained by eliminating a block), we can still correct a maximum of $\lfloor (d-1)/2 \rfloor$ errors in the overall received vector.

Let σ_i be the number of errors in the part of the received vector corresponding to the block C_i. We have to establish a procedure to recover $Z(u)$ from the received vector if,

$$\sum_{i=1}^{t+1} \sigma_i < \lfloor (d-1)/2 \rfloor$$

Once the decoding for each block C_i is performed, there are two

possibilities, namely:

(a) It is error free, i.e., $\sigma_i < \lfloor (\alpha_i-1)/2 \rfloor$

(b) It is incorrectly decoded, i.e., $\sigma_i > \lfloor (\alpha_i-1)/2 \rfloor$

Now, let the blocks C_{i_1}, C_{i_2}, ..., C_{i_f} be decoded incorrectly. The

least number of errors in the received vector for such an event to take

place is given by,

$$\min\{ \sum_{j=i_1,i_2,\ldots,i_f} \sigma_i \} = \sum_{j=i_1,i_2,\ldots,i_f} \{\lfloor (\alpha_j-1)/2 \rfloor + 1\}.$$

The decoder is to correct the errors for such an event only if,

$$\lfloor (d-1)/2 \rfloor > \sum_{j=i_1,i_2,\ldots,i_f} \{\lfloor (\alpha_j-1)/2 \rfloor + 1\}.$$

It is easy to show from the above that,

$$d > \sum_{j=i_1,i_2,\ldots,i_f} \alpha_j$$

or, alternatively,

$$\sum_{\substack{j=1}}^{t+1} \alpha_j > k \qquad\qquad\qquad (5.8)$$

$$j \neq i_1, i_2, \ldots, i_f$$

The above discussion can be summarised in the form of a theorem.

Theorem 5.1. If the number of errors that take place in a code vector

is less than $\lfloor (d-1)/2 \rfloor$, the error-correcting capability of the code,

then after each block C_i is decoded according to its minimum distance

α_i, there is <u>at least</u> one set of blocks which is error free such that the sum of the degrees of the polynomials $P_j(u)$ corresponding to these blocks is at least k. ∎

We will use this theorem for further analysis. Since the information vector is represented as a polynomial $Z(u)$ of degree $(k-1)$, it can be recovered using the CRT from any set of residues of the type,

$$Z_\ell(u) \equiv Z(u) \text{ modulo } P_\ell(u) \qquad \ell = \ell_1, \ell_2, \ldots$$

provided that,

$$\sum_{\ell = \ell_1, \ell_2, \ldots} \alpha_\ell > k$$

Let π be the set of integers $\pi = \{1, 2, \ldots, t+1\}$. The integer i in the set π corresponds to the polynomial $P_i(u)$ of degree α_i. The integer t+1 corresponds to the wraparound. From the above set, we form subsets of integers $\pi_1, \pi_2, \ldots$ such that each set is the <u>minimal</u> set with respect to the property that the sum of powers of the polynomials corresponding to the integers in each subset is at least k. Let this sum be k_1 for the subset π_1 and so on. Since $k_1 > k$, we can use the CRT to reconstruct a polynomial $Z_1'(u)$ of degree (k_1-1) using the residue polynomials $Z_\ell(u)$, $\ell \in \pi_1$. This procedure can also be performed for the subsets $\pi_2, \pi_3, \ldots$ and so on. If the reconstructed polynomial $Z_1'(u)$ for the subset π_1 is of degree (k_1-1), then, clearly, such a polynomial has to satisfy the following (k_1-k) equations for it to be accepted as a <u>candidate</u> for the transmitted polynomial

$$z_{1i}' = 0 \qquad i = k, k+1, \ldots, k_1-1, \qquad (5.9)$$

where

$$Z_1'(u) = z_{10}' + z_{11}'u + z_{12}'u^2 + \cdots + z_{1,k_1-1}'u^{k_1-1}.$$

Similar relationships hold for the remaining subsets $\pi_2, \ldots$.

Let $Z_1'(u)$, $Z_2'(u), \ldots$ be the <u>candidates</u> for the transmitted message polynomial. As the code under consideration has a minimum distance d, the code vector corresponding to a <u>valid</u> information polynomial will differ from the received vector in a maximum of $\lfloor (d-1)/2 \rfloor$ places. Theorem 5.1 guarantees the <u>existence</u> of at least one candidate information polynomial which is the valid information polynomial, provided the number of errors present in the received vector is less than the error-correcting capability of the code. Hence, if the code vector corresponding to a candidate information polynomial differs from the received vector in at most $\lfloor (d-1)/2 \rfloor$ places, it is accepted as the valid information polynomial.

The complete decoding algorithm for the codes may be enumerated as follows:

1. Partition the received vector according to blocks $C_1, C_2, \ldots C_{t+1}$ of C.

2. Perform the decoding for each block independently.

3. Discard the blocks for which a decoding failure takes place.

4. Using the CRT, construct the candidates for the information polynomial from the residue polynomials obtained from the blocks declared error-free in Step 3.

5. Construct the candidate code vectors for each of the candidate information polynomials.

6. Accept a candidate code vector as a valid code vector if it differs from the received vector in at most $\lfloor (d-1)/2 \rfloor$ places. The corresponding candidate information polynomial is then accepted as a valid information polynomial.

The Chinese remainder theorem establishes the uniqueness of the decoding procedure described above. A block diagram of the decoder is given in Figure 5.1. The decoding algorithm for each of the blocks is the same as the decoding algorithm described above, as these blocks are obtained from a computation of the same nature as the original code. Since each of the blocks is a code of small dimension and distance, as compared to the dimension and distance of the original code, we can examine these codes further to simplify the design of the decoder for these blocks. For example, the small (3,2,2), (6,3,3), and (9,4,4) codes are one-step majority logic decodable, and this fact can be incorporated into the design of the decoder for the blocks. Clearly, the decoder configuration is such that it can be implemented using parallel architecture, a feature which may be useful in high data rate communication systems. Furthermore, since codes of this type form the basis of the overall decoding procedure, it is plausible that the overall performance of the system may be improved by using soft-decision decoding for the small codes [22]. However, this issue will not be pursued further in this work.

Let us briefly analyse the complexity of the other blocks constituting the decoder. Consider the implementation for the recostruction for the set π_1. The set π_1 corresponds to the CRT reconstruction of the polynomial $Z_1'(u)$ of degree (k_1-1) from the knowledge of the residue polynomials $Z_\ell(u) \equiv Z(u)$ modulo $P_\ell(u)$, $\ell \in \pi_1$.

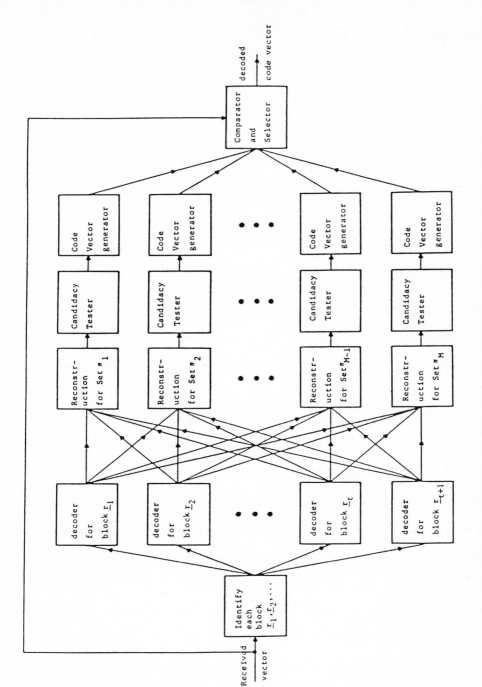

Figure 5.1. Block diagram for the decoder structure described in Section 5.2

Using the CRT, $Z_1'(u)$ is obtained as,

$$Z_1'(u) \equiv \sum_{\ell \in \pi_1} S_\ell(u) Z_\ell(u) \quad \text{modulo } P_1'(u) \tag{5.10}$$

where $P_1'(u) = \prod_{\ell \in \pi_1} P_\ell(u)$.

The polynomials $S_\ell(u)$ are determined a priori from the knowledge of $P_\ell(u)$, $\ell \in \pi_1$. The expression (5.10) can be implemented in three steps as follows:

    (i)   Compute $S_\ell(u) Z_\ell(u)$, $\ell \in \pi_1$.

    (ii)   Form the sum $\sum_{\ell \in \pi_1} S_\ell(u) Z_\ell(u)$.

    (iii) Reduce the resulting polynomial modulo $P_1'(u)$.

Step (i) can be implemented by a multiplication circuit as shown in Figure 5.2 [9]. Step (ii) is implemented using a series of adders, one for every coefficient. Note that adders are equivalent to exclusive-OR gates over GF(2). Step (iii) is implemented by the feedback shift-register configuration shown in Figure 4.2. The reconstruction for the sets π_2, π_3.... can be implemented in a similar manner. A shift-register based implementation of the codevector generator was discussed in Section 4.3. Finally, the implementation of the candidacy tester and the comparator and selector blocks is clear from the description of the decoding algorithm.

Also consider the decoder design when k is increased (decreased), keeping the length of the code n constant. Steps 1,2, and 3 of the decoding algorithm are unaltered. The decoder circuit for Step 4 of the algorithm has to be suitably modified. It has been shown in Chapter 4 that a change in k does not imply a significant change in the encoding

71

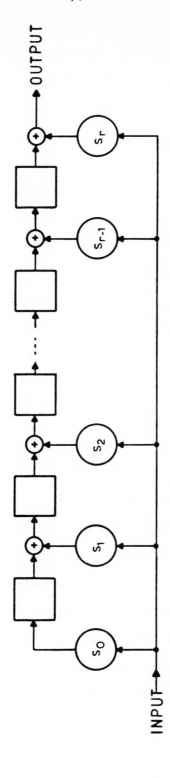

Figure 5.2. A shift-register circuit for multiplication by a polynomial

$$S(u) = s_0 + s_1 u + \ldots + s_r u^r$$

procedure, and therefore, Step 5 does not involve a significant change as k is varied. In Step 6, we only have to adjust the threshold of the comparator to the error-correcting capability, $\lfloor (d-1)/2 \rfloor$, of the new code. In the following, we present two examples to illustrate the decoding algorithm developed above.

Example 1. Consider the (8,4,3) code. P(u) is chosen as
$P(u) = u(u^2+1)(u^2+u+1)$, and s = 1. The received vector is partitioned into four blocks C_1, C_2, C_3, and C_4 corresponding to $P_1(u) = u$, $P_2(u) = (u^2+1)$, $P_3(u) = (u^2+u+1)$, and the wraparound, respectively. The blocks C_1 and C_4 are (1,1,1) codes for which no decoder is required. The decoder for blocks C_2 and C_3 is a decoder for the (3,2,2) code and simply checks the block for even parity. If this test fails, the block is rejected. The set π is given by,

$$\pi = \{1,2,3,4\}$$

with possible subsets,

$$\pi_1 = \{1,2,4\}$$
$$\pi_2 = \{2,3\}$$
$$\pi_3 = \{1,3,4\}$$

The subsets π_1, π_2, and π_3 correspond to different choices of the residue polynomials that can be used to recover the information polynomial. No candidacy tester and comparator are required for the subsets. If we are interested only in the recovery of the information polynomial, the code vector generator is also not required in this case. A circuit diagram for the resulting decoder is given in Figure 5.3. The generator matrix of the code is derived in Section 4.1.

Example 2. Consider the (24,6,9) code. The polynomials are $P_1(u) = u^2$,

73

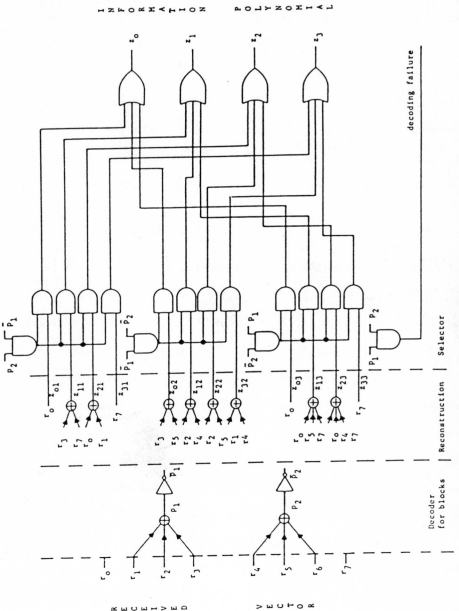

Figure 5.3. Decoder circuit for (8,4,3) binary code

$P_2(u) = (u^2+u+1)$, $P_3(u) = (u^2+1)$, $P_4(u) = (u^3+u+1)$, $P_5(u) = (u^3+u^2+1)$

and s = 2. The received vector is to be partitioned into 6 blocks

C_1, C_2,..., C_6 corresponding to the polynomials $P_1(u)$,..., $P_5(u)$, and

the wraparound, respectively. The blocks C_1, C_2, C_3, C_6 are (3,2,2)

codes and blocks C_4, C_5 are (6,3,3) codes. Therefore, decoders for

blocks C_1, C_2, C_3, and C_6 are simple parity checks and a block is

rejected if it has odd parity. The decoders for blocks C_4 and C_5 are

identical. This decoder is a one-step majority logic decoder. The set

π is,

$$\pi = \{1,2,3,4,5,6\}$$

and there are 17 possible subsets given by, $\pi_1 = \{4,5\}$, $\pi_2 = \{1,2,3\}$,

$\pi_3 = \{2,3,6\}$, $\pi_4 = \{1,2,6\}$, $\pi_5 = \{1,3,6\}$, $\pi_6 = \{1,2,4\}$, $\pi_7 = \{1,3,4\}$,

$\pi_8 = \{1,4,6\}$, $\pi_9 = \{2,3,4\}$, $\pi_{10} = \{2,4,6\}$, $\pi_{11} = \{3,4,6\}$, $\pi_{12} = \{1,2,5\}$,

$\pi_{13} = \{1,3,5\}$, $\pi_{14} = \{1,5,6\}$, $\pi_{15} = \{2,3,5\}$, $\pi_{16} = \{2,5,6\}$, and $\pi_{17} = \{3,5,6\}$.

For a parallel implementation, the decoder requires 17 blocks for

reconstruction of the polynomials to be tested for candidacy. The

candidacy tester is present only for the subsets π_6, π_7,..., π_{17}. The

code vector generator is not enabled if the candidacy tester fails. The

comparator is a set of 24 exclusive-OR gates followed by a counter and a

threshold detector set at 5.

Given the decoder for the (24,6,9) code, let us analyse the

overhead required to decode the (24,8,7) code. The design of the

decoder for the blocks C_1, C_2,..., C_6 is unaltered. There are 13

subsets for the (24,8,7) code given by, $\pi_1 = \{1,2,3,6\}$, $\pi_2 = \{1,2,3,4\}$,

$\pi_3 = \{2,3,4,6\}$, $\pi_4 = \{1,2,4,6\}$ $\pi_5 = \{1,3,4,6\}$, $\pi_6 = \{1,2,3,5\}$,

$\pi_7 = \{2,3,5,6\}$, $\pi_8 = \{1,2,5,6\}$, $\pi_9 = \{1,3,5,6\}$, $\pi_{10} = \{1,4,5\}$,

$\pi_{11} = \{2,4,5\}$, $\pi_{12} = \{3,4,5\}$, $\pi_{13} = \{4,5,6\}$ and we require 13 reconstruction blocks. The subsets π_1, π_{10}, π_{11}, π_{12} and π_{13} do not require a candidacy test. The design of the code vector generator and the comparator is essentially as before, except that the threshold detector is now set at 4.

5.3   Experimental Results

Since majority logic decoding is a simple method of determining the error digits from the parity check sums, we examined the majority logic decodability of a larger number of linear codes belonging to this new class of linear codes. The reader is referred to [8] for a detailed description of majority logic decoding of linear codes.

At the receiving end, we are generally interested in reliably recovering only the information symbols, therefore, we restrict our attention to finding orthogonal check sums on the error digits that correspond to the message digits. The following definition characteristics the majority logic decodability of linear codes.

Definition.   A linear code with minimum distance d is said to be sufficiently orthogonalisable in one step iff it is possible to form $J = d-1$ parity check sums orthogonal on each of the error digits that correspond to the message digits. For a code that is sufficiently orthogonalisable, we can estimate the message vector correctly even if $\lfloor (d-1)/2 \rfloor$ errors take place in the received vector. We also note that a completely orthogonalisable code is always sufficiently orthogonalisable, but the converse may not be true.

In our analysis, the following codes were found to be sufficiently orthogonalisable in one step.

(i)   (6,3,3)   1 error-correcting

(ii)   (8,4,3)   1 error-correcting

(iii)   (10,5,3)   1 error-correcting

(iv)   (10,3,5)   2 error-correcting

(v)   (12,6,3)   1 error-correcting

(vi)   (12,4,5)   2 error-correcting

(vii)   (14,3,7)   3 error-correcting

(viii) (14,5,5)   2 error-correcting

(ix)   (16,4,7)   3 error-correcting

(x)   (16,6,5)   2 error-correcting

(xi)   (18,5,7)   3 error-correcting

(xii)   (18,3,9)   4 error-correcting

(xiii) (20,4,9)   4 error-correcting

(xiv)   (22,5,9)   4 error-correcting

(xv)   (22,3,11)   5 error-correcting

(xvi)   (24,4,11)   5 error-correcting

(xvii) (26,5,11)   5 error-correcting

(xviii) (30,5,13)   6 error-correcting

Also, the (24,6,9) code was found to be a 2-step sufficiently orthogonalizable code. The parity check equations for the above listed codes are given in Appendix B.

5.4   Code Family Relationships for Encoding/Decoding

It has been shown that the encoding/decoding methods utilise the block structure of the codes, arising due to the computation $Z_i(u)Y_i(u)$ modulo the relatively prime factor polynomials $P_i(u)$, $i = 1,2,\ldots t$ and the wraparound of s points. Such a structure can be used to advantage

to design codes with the same dimension k, but different minimum
distance d. In this section, we analyse the block structure of the
generator matrix and show that it is possible to obtain a group of codes
of dimension k, having different error correcting capability, in a way
that the encoder/decoder design for this group of codes is essentially
the same. Such codes may find application in communication systems that
employ variable redundancy codes for adaptive error-correction [29].

For the computation of an aperiodic convolution of length N =
k+d-1, the degree D of the polynomial P(u) and the number of wraparound
points s satisfy the relation,

$$N = k+d-1 = D+s \qquad (5.11)$$

If the polynomial P(u) has t relatively prime polynomial factors, $P_i(u)$,
each of degree α_i, then,

$$D = \sum_{i=1}^{t} \alpha_i \qquad (5.12)$$

Combining (5.11) and (5.12), we obtain,

$$k+d-1 = \sum_{i=1}^{t+1} \alpha_i, \qquad (5.13)$$

where $\alpha_{t+1} = s$. Based on (5.13), we state the following lemma:

Lemma 5.2. If the block C_j corresponding to the computation

$\Phi_j(u) \equiv Z_j(u)Y_j(u)$ modulo $P_j(u)$ is deleted from C, the resulting matrix

is a $(n-n_j, k, d-\alpha_j)$ code.

Proof. Equation (5.13) can be written in the form,

$$k + (d - \sum_{j=i_1,i_2,\ldots} \alpha_j) - 1 = \sum_{\substack{i=1 \\ i \neq i_1,i_2,\ldots}}^{t+1} \alpha_i \qquad (5.14)$$

The length of the code is equal to the sum total of the complexity associated with each block, that is,

$$n = \sum_{i=1}^{t+1} M(\alpha_i)$$

In accordance with (5.14), the above equation can be written as,

$$n - \sum_{j=i_1, i_2, \ldots} M(\alpha_j) = \sum_{\substack{i=1 \\ i \neq i_1, i_2, \ldots}}^{t+1} M(\alpha_i) \qquad (5.15)$$

Equation (5.14) indicates that it is possible to obtain a code of dimension k and distance d' from a given code of dimension k and distance d(d' < d) by discarding the computation with regard to the factor polynomials $P_j(u)$, $j = i_1, i_2, \ldots$ such that,

$$d' = d - \sum_{j=i_1, i_2, \ldots} \alpha_j$$

while (5.15) indicates that the generator matrix of such a code is obtained by simply __dropping__ the columns of the original generator matrix belonging to the blocks C_j, $j = i_1, i_2, \ldots$ and also establishes the length n' of the new code. ∎

Hence, by using Lemma 5.2, the generator matrix C' of the (n',k,d') code is obtained from the generator matrix C of the (n,k,d) code by appropriately deleting columns of C. For a given value of d', the various α_j, $j = i_1, i_2, \ldots$ are chosen so as to minimise n'. Such a choice then leads to the most efficient code possible for this procedure.

Let us consider the (24,6,9) code to illustrate this unique feature of these linear codes. The various polynomials are $P_1(u) = u^2$, $P_2(u) = (u^2+u+1)$, $P_3(u) = (u^2+1)$, $P_4(u) = (u^3+u+1)$, $P_5(u) = (u^3+u^2+1)$ and

$s = 2$. The generator matrix for this code has 6 blocks. From the (24,6,9) code, we can obtain the (21,6,7) code by dropping any one of the 4 blocks (having 3 columns each) C_1, C_2, C_3, or C_6 from the generator matrix of the (24,6,9) code. Using similar techniques, we can obtain the generator matrices for the (18,6,6), (15,6,4), and (12,6,3) codes by discarding suitable groups of columns from the generator matrix C of the (24,6,9) code.

Given the decoder of an (n,k,d) code, we now consider the problem of designing a decoder for the (n',k,d') code obtained by dropping blocks $\{C_J\} = \{C_j, j = i_1, i_2, \ldots\}$ from the generator matrix C of the (n,k,d) code. The blocks present in the resulting (n',k,d') code are also present in the original (n,k,d) code and, therefore, Steps 1, 2, and 3 of the decoding procedure described in Section 5.2 are <u>unaltered</u>. The decoders for the blocks $\{C_J\}$ are simply disabled. In Step 4 of the procedure, the reconstruction for a subset π_β is disabled if the subset π_β has any of the decoder outputs corresponding to the blocks $\{C_J\}$ as input. The reconstruction for the remaining subsets is the same as that of the (n,k,d) code. In Step 5, the outputs of the code vector generator corresponding to the blocks $\{C_J\}$ are again disabled, so as to obtain the code vectors of length n'. In Step 6, the threshold of the comparator is now set at $\lfloor (d'-1)/2 \rfloor$, the error-correcting capability of the new code.

Since the (n',k,d') code is a lower minimum distance code as compared to the (n,k,d) code, it is expected that the decoder structure for the (n',k,d') code be simpler than the (n,k,d) code, which is indeed the case. It is clear from the above description that the decoder for the (n',k,d') code is obtained by simply disabling a part of the decoder for the (n,k,d) code. As a result, the processing througput of the decoder for all such codes is the same.

For example, consider the decoder design for the (21,6,7) code obtained from the (24,6,9) code by dropping the block C_1. Therefore, $\{C_J\} = \{C_1\}$ and, consequently, the decoder for the block C_1 is disabled in Step 1. In Step 4, the reconstruction for the subsets π_2, π_4, π_5, π_6, π_7, π_8, π_{12}, π_{13}, and π_{14} are disabled, as all these subsets have the output of the decoder for the block C_1 as one of their inputs. Note that this also reduces the number of comparisons to be performed at the final stage of the decoding procedure. For the (21,6,7) code, the threshold of the comparator is reduced to 4 in Step 6.

A similar approach can be adopted to obtain an (n',k,d') code from an (n,k,d) code when d' > d. In this case, groups of columns are appended to the generator matrix of the (n,k,d) code. Every new group of columns corresponds to a computation with regard to a new polynomial $P_j(u)$. However, care must be taken that the polynomial $P_j(u)$ be <u>coprime</u> to all the existing polynomials $P_i(u)$, i = 1,2,..., t. The decoder structure for such a code can be easily analysed. It is worthwhile to observe that the decoder would be more complex in design and require additional hardware; however, the additional processing requirements can easily be determined due to the <u>highly</u> <u>structured</u>, <u>systematic</u> decoding procedure shown in Figure 5.1.

5.5 Burst Error-Detection Capability

In this section, a procedure is outlined which can be used to determine the burst error-detection capability of the codes under investigation. The information vector can be expressed as a polynomial Z(u) of degree (k-1). Consider the polynomial $Z_i(u)$ obtained as,

$$Z_i(u) \equiv Z(u) \quad \text{modulo } P_i(u).$$

Clearly, $Z_i(u)$ is zero iff $Z(u)$ is a multiple of $P_i(u)$. Consequently, if $Z(u)$ is a multiple of $P_i(u)$, then the block corresponding to the computation,

$$\Phi_i(u) \equiv Z_i(u)Y_i(u) \quad \text{modulo } P_i(u) \tag{5.16}$$

is zero. Let the blocks corresponding to C_{i_1}, C_{i_2} be zero in a codevector. Since $Z(u)$ is a degree $(k-1)$ polynomial, the following constraint must be satisfied for the blocks C_{i_1}, C_{i_2},...,

$$\sum_{i=i_1,i_2\ldots} \alpha_i \leqslant k-1 \ .$$

Also, $$\sum_{i=1}^{t+1} \alpha_i = k+d-1.$$

Combining the above two expressions, we obtain,

$$\sum_{i\neq i_1,i_2,\ldots} \alpha_i \ \geqslant d \ .$$

This discussion can be summarised in the form of a lemma as follows:

Lemma 5.3. for any arbitrary information vector, the sum of the degrees of the polynomials $P_i(u)$ such that the associated blocks of the codevector are nonzero, is at least d.   ∎

Conversely, if there is a vector having nonzero elements corresponding to C_{i_1}, C_{i_2},..., and

$$\alpha_{i_1} + \alpha_{i_2} +\ldots < d \ , \tag{5.17}$$

then, such a vector cannot be a codevector. We, further, assume that the computation (5.16) is performed in such a way that each of the blocks C_i is an $(n_i, \alpha_i, \alpha_i)$ code. Therefore, for every codevector the number of nonzero elements in a nonzero block is at least α_i.

The Lemma 5.3 and the above stated assumption can be used to determine the burst error-detection capability of the codes. For example, for the (24,6,9) code, if blocks C_1, C_2,..., C_6 correspond to $P_1(u) = u^2$, $P_2(u) = (u^2+1)$, $P_3(u) = (u^3+u+1)$, $P_4(u) = (u^2+u+1)$, $P_5(u) = (u^3+u^2+1)$, and the wraparound s = 2, then it can be shown that the code can detect error bursts of length upto 12.

Unfortunately, the burst error-detection capability for these codes depends on the ordering of the blocks and, therefore, it is not possible to derive a closed form expression as is true in the case of cyclic codes.

DISCUSSION OF RESULTS: PART ONE

As described in Chapters 3 and 4, it is clear from the construction of the aperiodic convolution algorithm that the associated multiplicative complexity is directly dependent upon the complexities of the
polynomial multiplication algorithms and the choice of the modulo polynomial $P(u)$. A number of algorithms are possible and in this work effort
is directed towards construction of algorithms with as low a multiplicative complexity as possible, for the reasons given earlier. The formul-
ation of the problem is such that the additive complexity of the algorithms does not play any role in the design of the algorithms. The
examples presented in Chapter 4 illustrate that a wide variety of
algorithms may be generated.

It is of interest to compare the actual complexity of the
aperiodic convolution algorithm to its theoretical lower bound. If
$P_i(u) = Q_i^{\beta_i}(u)$, and $Q_i(u)$ is irreducible over F, then the minimum number
of multiplications required to compute $\Phi_i(u) = Z_i(u)Y_i(u)$ modulo $P_i(u)$
is $2\alpha_i - 1$, where deg $[P_i(u)] = \alpha_i$ [11]. This result can be extended to
obtain a lower bound on the multiplicative complexity of the CRT based
procedure to compute the aperiodic convolution of length N. If $P(u)$ has
t factors and the wraparound of $s(s \geqslant 1)$ coefficients is used to compute
$\Phi(u) = Z(u)Y(u)$, then the lower bound on the multiplicative complexity
of the procedure (and the length of the associated code) is $n_{min} =$
$2N-(t+1)$. For example, for $N = 14$, $P(u) = u^2(u^2+u+1)(u^2+1)(u^3+u+1)$
(u^3+u^2+1), $s = 2$, and therefore, $n_{min} = 28-6 = 22$. This compares
favourably with the actual complexity of the aperiodic convolution

algorithm of length 14 which is 24. We are not familiar with any meaningful upperbound on the complexity of the aperiodic convolution algorithm except for the trivial bound which states that the product of two polynomials of degrees k-1 and d-1, can be computed in kd multiplications.

It has been shown that a bilinear algorithm over GF(p) which is valid for input data over GF(p) is also valid for input data over $GF(p^m)$ [21]. Hence, the results of this paper, including the technique to design the bilinear algorithm, remain valid even if the prime 2 is replaced everywhere by a power of 2. This increases the field of constants and this fact can be further incorporated into the design of the algorithm, thereby reducing the multiplicative complexity and, hence, reducing the length of the codes over $GF(2^m)$.

The linear codes obtained from the algorithms compare well with similar codes which are already known in terms of their rate and distance properties. The complexity of the decoding algorithm presented in Chapter 5 is in direct proportion to the number of relatively prime factors of the polynomial P(u). A large number of such factors increases the complexity of the decoder while minimising the overall length of the code for a prespecified value of k and d. Hence, a tradeoff is possible between the complexity of the decoder and the length of the code.

Another interesting feature of the decoding algorithm is that it uses small length codes as a basis for the decoding of a large length code. The design of the decoder for the codes of small length and distance is very simple as compared to a large length code. Because of this modular structure, the decoder can also detect and correct several

error patterns having Hamming weight greater than the error-correcting
capability of the code. For example, the decoder circuit of the (8,4,3)
code given in Figure 5.3, can detect 32 percent of all the possible
error patterns of Hamming weight 2. Also a large number of these codes
were found to be one step majority logic decodable.

Among the binary codes generated from the aperiodic convolution
algorithms, a large number of these codes were analysed with the help of
the computer in order to determine the actual minimum distance of the
code as compared to the designed minimum distance. The actual minimum
distance of most of the codes tested was found to be the <u>same</u> as the
designed minimum distance. Also, the weight distribution of a selected
number of codes is given in Appendix C.

PART II

APPLICATIONS TO DIGITAL

COMMUNICATION SYSTEMS

CHAPTER 6

AUTOMATIC REPEAT REQUEST SYSTEMS

There are two fundamental techniques for error control in digital communication systems: Forward Error Control (FEC) schemes and Automatic Repeat Request (ARQ) schemes [9]. In a digital communication system using FEC, the transmitter employs an error-correcting code to add redundant digits to the information digits in a manner so as to correct the error patterns that are most likely to occur during transmission. At the receiving end, the decoder attempts to recover the information digits from the received digits in a way so as to maximise a certain system performance measure.

In digital communication systems using ARQ, the data to be transmitted are first organised in blocks after which an error-detecting code is used to encode each block in order to achieve the required error-detection capability. No error-correction is performed by the receiver. When an error is detected in a block, a request for retransmission is made through a reverse (or feedback) channel. The transmitter is informed of whether a block is correctly or incorrectly received by an acknowledgement (ACK) or nonacknowledgement (NACK), respectively. If an ACK is received at the transmitter, a new block is transmitted; whereas, if a NACK is received, the same block is transmitted again. With this procedure a block is delivered to the user only when no errors are detected by the receiver.

Both of these error-control schemes, FEC and ARQ, have their relative advantages and disadvantages. An important measure of performance of such systems is their throughput efficiency [23]. The throughput efficiency is defined as the ratio of the number of information bits to the total number of bits transmitted. Since there are no retransmissions in a FEC system, the information throughput efficiency is constant and set by the code rate, regardless of the channel transmission conditions. The most severe drawback of an ARQ system is its throughput efficiency. The information throughput of an ARQ system depends strongly on the number of requested retransmissions, that is, on channel quality and therefore falls rapidly with increasing channel error rate [24,25,26].

Another important measure of performance is the system reliability. Reliability is measured by the probability of the event that the transmitted code vector and the vector accepted by the receiver as an estimate of the transmitted code vector are not the same. In FEC systems, the reliability of the received data is very sensitive to any degradation in the channel conditions and the selection of an appropriate error-correcting code depends on the detailed knowledge of the error statistics of the channel [9]. By using a proper error-detecting code, the probability of undetected error can be made very small [8]. As the probability of a decoding error for an error-correcting code is much greater than the probability of undetected error, the ARQ systems are far more reliable than FEC systems. Furthermore, a code used for error-detection is not very sensitive to the actual error patterns, and it can detect the vast majority of the error patterns. Consequently, unlike FEC systems, the use of ARQ error control is effective on most channels.

The cost of an ARQ system is also substantially lower than that of a FEC system. This is due to the fact that error-detection is, by its nature, a much simpler task than error-correction. In addition error-detection with retransmission is adaptive, i.e., transmission of redundant information is increased when errors occur. This makes it possible under certain circumstances to get better performance with an ARQ system than is theoretically possible with a FEC system.

From the above discussion, it is clear that the ARQ scheme can provide high system reliability reasonably independently of the channel quality. However, as the channel becomes noisier, the requests for retransmission increase, leading to a reduced throughput. On the other hand, FEC techniques provide a constant throughput regardless of the channel quality, but the system reliability will fall as the channel degrades.

In situations where the channel error rate is too high to guarantee desired throughput using ARQ and where the required system reliability is too high to be achieved by FEC alone, a combination of FEC and ARQ systems may be attractive. Such a scheme is termed as hybrid ARQ [8,27]. In principle, the hybrid scheme combines the advantages of both techniques. A combination of correction of the most frequent error patterns (FEC) and detection coupled with retransmission for less frequent error patterns (ARQ) provides high throughput efficiency as well as high system reliability.

It was shown in Chapter 5 that the class of linear error-correcting codes derived from the aperiodic convolution algorithm using the CRT is characterised by modular structure which, in turn, can be used to design codes with variable minimum distance having the same encoding/decoding procedure. In Part II of this work, this class of linear codes is proposed as an excellent candidate for the hybrid ARQ application [28].

6.1 Basic ARQ System

In this section, we describe the three basic types of ARQ schemes that can be used for error control in digital communication systems. This is followed by a brief analysis of their relative efficiencies and the complexity of the system required to implement them.

There are three basic ARQ schemes:

1. Stop-and-Wait ARQ

2. Go-back N or Continuous ARQ

3. Selective-Repeat ARQ

Stop-and-Wait ARQ. This is the simplest of the three ARQ techniques. In this scheme, a block is transmitted and a copy of it stored in the transmitter buffer. The next block is not transmitted until an ACK is received; one or more NACK's simply result in retransmission of the buffer contents. Such a scheme is shown in Figure 6.1. The transmitter idle time is at least equal to the round-trip delay time.

Go-back N or Continuous ARQ. In Go-back N or continuous ARQ systems, the blocks are transmitted in order over the channel without waiting for an ACK/NACK response. The transmitter buffer is now larger, holding a number of consecutive blocks with total length equal approximately to the ratio of round-trip delay to block time-duration or N. The ACK or NACK for a block arrives after a round-trip delay. Whenever a NACK is received by the transmitter, the buffer is accessed with the entire contents transmitted in order to preserve the natural ordering of the blocks. At the receiver, the erroneously received block and all the N-1 succeeding blocks are discarded. Retransmissions continue until the

93

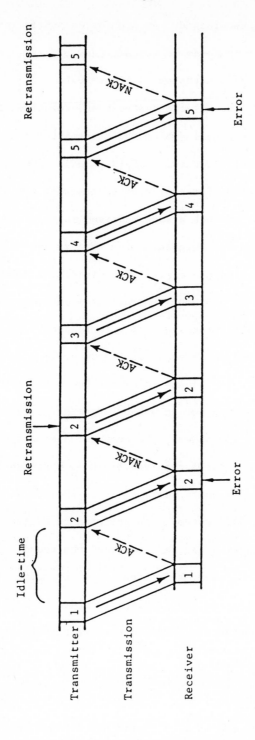

Figure 6.1. Stop-and-Wait ARQ scheme

block is positively acknowledged. As soon as an ACK is received for the block, the transmitter proceeds to transmit new blocks. The basic go-back-N ARQ scheme is illustrated in Figure 6.2.

Selective-Repeat ARQ. The Selective-Repeat ARQ technique is a variation of the continuous ARQ scheme in which the transmitter resends only those blocks that are negatively acknowledged (NACK'ed). After resending a NACK'ed block, the transmitter continues to transmit new blocks. However, as the blocks are not always received in consecutive order by the receiver, more complex logic and large buffers are required. When the first NACK'ed block is successfully received, the receiver releases any error-free blocks in consecutive order from the receiver buffer until the next erroneously received block is reached. The selective-repeat ARQ scheme is shown in Figure 6.3.

The stop-and-wait ARQ scheme is simple but inefficient because of the idle time spent waiting for an acknowledgement of each transmitted block. In a go-back N ARQ scheme, the receiver also rejects the next N-1 received blocks whenever a received block is detected in error. Consequently, they must also be retransmitted, thereby reducing the efficiency of the overall system. The performance of these two ARQ schemes depends strongly on the data rate and the round-trip delay. For a selective-repeat ARQ system, sufficient receiver buffer storage (theoretically infinite) must be provided in order to assemble the received blocks in consecutive order, otherwise buffer overflow may occur and the blocks lost.

6.2 Hybrid ARQ Schemes

In this section, the various hybrid ARQ schemes that can be used for error control are presented and their main features are highlighted.

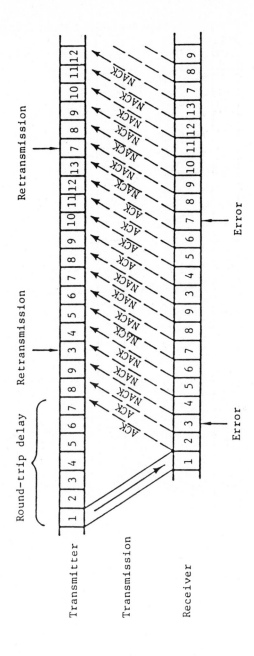

Figure 6.2. Go-back-N or Continuous ARQ scheme (N=7)

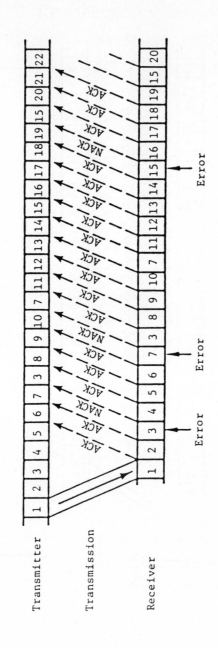

Figure 6.3. Selective-Repeat ARQ scheme

There are a number of factors that require analysis in order to select an appropriate scheme for the error control problem. The main factors are the channel characteristics and the cost and complexity of the system required to implement the scheme.

As it was stated earlier, hybrid ARQ schemes can be used to overcome the drawbacks of the FEC and the ARQ systems. Such schemes can be broadly classed as [24]:

1. Type- I Hybrid ARQ Schemes

2. Type-II Hybrid ARQ Schemes

6.2.1 Type-I hybrid ARQ schemes

A type-I hybrid ARQ scheme employs a code for error-correction (FEC) and error-detection (ARQ) as shown in Figure 6.4. At the receiver, the decoder first attempts to correct the received block. Then, the decoded block is checked for error-detection. If an uncorrectable error pattern is detected, the received block is rejected and a NACK is sent to the transmitter. The transmitter, upon receiving a NACK, retransmits the same block. This procedure is continued until the block is successfully accepted by the receiver. In this technique, an erroneous block is delivered to the user only if error patterns in the decoded block cannot be detected by the error-detecting code.

Since a type-I ARQ scheme uses codes for error-correction as well as error-detection, it requires more parity check bits than a code used for error-detection alone as in the ARQ schemes discussed in Section 6.1. Consequently, for good channels, the throughput of a type-I hybrid ARQ scheme may be lower than that of the corresponding ARQ scheme. However, when the channel error rate is high, a type-I hybrid ARQ scheme provides higher throughput than the corresponding ARQ scheme, because its error-correcting code is designed to correct the most frequently

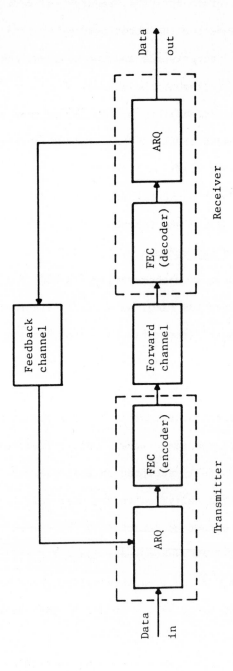

Figure 6.4. A Type-I hybrid ARQ scheme

occurring channel error patterns. For this reason, type-I hybrid ARQ
schemes are best suited for communication over channels whose
characteristics are known a priori to be fairly constant.

For communication systems in which the channel characteristics
change, a type-I hybrid ARQ system may not be very efficient. When the
channel is quiet (that is, errors are introduced very infrequently), no
error-correction is required and, therefore, the extra parity-check bits
for error-correction included in each block are not needed. When the
channel is noisy (that is, the errors are introduced frequently), the
error-correcting code may become inadequate. This, in turn, increases
retransmissions, thus lowering the throughput. It can alternately be
argued that it is difficult in practice to design good error-correcting
codes for channels having varying characteristics. An example of such a
channel is the satellite channel which is very quiet in good weather and
behaves poorly during rain.

6.2.2 Type-II hybrid ARQ schemes

For a channel having non-stationary behaviour, it might be
desirable to utilise an adaptive hybrid ARQ scheme. Error-detection
with retransmission is adaptive, i.e., transmission of redundant
information is increased when errors occur. This forms the basis of
type-II hybrid ARQ schemes. The concept of variable redundancy codes
was first introduced by Mandelbaum [29] and based on this concept, a
type-II hybrid ARQ scheme was proposed by Metzner [30,31], Lin et al
[24], and Wang et al [32].

In the type-II hybrid ARQ system, the parity check bits for error-
correction are sent to the receiver only when they are needed. The
type-II hybrid scheme uses two linear codes denoted by V_0 and V_1, where

V_0 is an (n,k) error-detecting code and V_1 is a (2n,n) half-rate invertible code, designed for error-correction only. A (2n,n) code is said to be an invertible code if, knowing only the n parity-check bits of a codeword, the associated n information bits can be uniquely determined by an inversion process.

Let I denote the block of length n formed on the basis of the message D of length k and the (n,k) code V_0. Corresponding to the block I, a parity block P(I), also of length n, is formed using I and the code V_1. Now, I is transmitted; the corresponding received block is denoted by $\tilde{I}$. When $\tilde{I}$ is received, the receiver attempts to detect the presence of errors using V_0. If no errors are detected, $\tilde{I}$ is assumed error-free, and an ACK is sent to the transmitter. If the presence of errors is detected by V_0, the received block is stored in a buffer and a NACK is sent.

Upon receiving a NACK, the transmitter sends the parity block, P(I); the corresponding received block is denoted by $\tilde{P}(I)$. When $\tilde{P}(I)$ is received, the receiver takes the inverse of $\tilde{P}(I)$, denoted by $I(\tilde{P})$, based on V_1. If $\tilde{P}(I)$ is error-free, $I(\tilde{P})$ is the same as the original block I and is a codeword in V_0. Therefore, once $I(\tilde{P})$ is calculated, the receiver attempts to detect errors in $I(\tilde{P})$ based on V_0. If no errors are detected, $I(\tilde{P})$ is assumed error-free and an ACK is sent. If errors are detected in $I(\tilde{P})$, then the blocks $\tilde{P}(I)$ and $\tilde{I}$ are used together for error-correction based on the (2n,n) code V_1. Let $\hat{I}$ denote the decoded block after the error-correction process. Now, $\hat{I}$ is checked based on V_0. If no errors are detected, then $\hat{I}$ is assumed error-free and an ACK is sent. If errors are detected in $\hat{I}$, the receiver discards the block $\tilde{I}$, stores the block $\tilde{P}(I)$, and sends a NACK. The second retransmission is the block I itself. The error detection/correction procedure is then repeated. The retransmissions continue until the block is successfully received. The retransmissions are alternate repetitions of the block I and the parity block $P(I)$.

Depending on the choice of the error-correcting code V_1, two variations of the above scheme are available. In [30], Metzner proposed a scheme wherein small subblocks of the original n-bit block are taken to be the data bits of a rate one-half code. The choices for the code are stated to be limited to the (6,3,3), (8,4,4) Reed-Muller, and (16,8,5) codes. In [32], Wang et al described a scheme wherein the code V_1 operates on the complete data block and, consequently, it is a code having large length, dimension, and distance properties. It is worthwhile to mention here that for ARQ applications, a large value (n ~ 500) is usually selected for n [24].

It is clear from the above description that the overall performance of the type-II hybrid ARQ system depends very strongly on the choice of the error-correcting code V_1. In this respect, the scheme performs better for the codes given in [32] as compared to the subblock encoding approach of [30]. However, the complexity of decoding a large (2n,n) code is much greater than the complexity of decoding a small code. In addition, long codes must decode after hard digit decisions, whereas soft-decision decoding of block codes can be used to make a combined hard decision for each of the subblocks in the subblock encoding approach. Furthermore, since long codes generally have large decoding delays, it may not be feasible to use such a code in high data rate communication systems.

In Figure 6.5, typical plots of throughput efficiency versus channel bit error rate for the selective-repeat, type-I, and type-II hybrid selective-repeat ARQ schemes are presented for comparison [23]. It can be observed from the figure that the throughput of selective-repeat and type-II hybrid ARQ schemes is constant (and, close to 1) for the channel error rate upto 10^{-5} while the throughput of the type-I hybrid ARQ scheme is constant (though, less than 1) for channel error rate upto 10^{-4}. Also, the throughput of the selective-repeat ARQ and the type-I hybrid ARQ technique decreases rapidly as the channel begins to degrade, while the throughput of the type-II technique falls less rapidly as it approaches 0.5. In fact, the throughput has an inflection at 0.5 for the type-II hybrid ARQ scheme. This is due to the reason that error-correction is performed upon the first retransmission in type-II hybrid ARQ system, and therefore, the probability of further retransmissions is considerably reduced.

In the next chapter, the above described type-II hybrid ARQ scheme is generalized. Such a generalized scheme utilises the redundancy available upon successive retransmission in a more efficient manner, and, consequently, leads to higher throughput of the ARQ scheme in situations when the channel error rate is high.

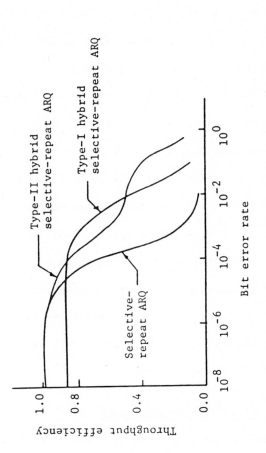

Figure 6.5. Throughput efficiency of various ARQ schemes

CHAPTER 7

A GENERALIZED TYPE-II HYBRID ARQ SCHEME

In this chapter, we generalize the type-II hybrid ARQ scheme described in Chapter 6, Section 6.2.2. It has been stated earlier that
error-detection with retransmission is adaptive. The first retransmission of a block provides the receiver with n redundant digits and
this forms the basis of the type-II hybrid ARQ scheme of the previous
section. A natural question arises at this stage: 'What is the optimal
way of using the redundant information when more than one retransmission
is requested?'. For example, in the type-II ARQ scheme, the second
retransmission is the same as the information block. Clearly, the
performance of the system can be further improved if the second
retransmission is another parity block which may be used to form a
(3n,n) error-correcting code. Such a scheme can be generalized to any
number of parity blocks before the transmitter resends the blocks in
repetition once again. We will refer to this scheme as a Generalized
Type-II Hybrid ARQ (GH-ARQ) scheme.

7.1 Description of the GH-ARQ Scheme

The GH-ARQ scheme also uses two codes; one is a high rate (n,k)
code V_0 which is designed for error-detection only, and the second is
the code V_1 which is used adaptively for error-correction. The code V_1
is an (mn,n) error-correcting code having distance d, selected in a way
that its generator matrix can be partitioned into m subblocks each of
dimension $(n \times n)$. The integer m will be referred to as the __depth__ of the
code. Let the generator matrix of V_1 be denoted by G and the subblocks
of G be denoted by $G_1, G_2, \ldots, G_m$. Then, G can be written as,

$$G = [G_1 \mid G_2 \mid \cdots \mid G_m].$$ (7.1)

For the code V_1 to be useful for the application under consideration, it is assumed that subcode $V_1^{(i)}$ with the generator matrix $G^{(i)}$, where $G^{(i)} = [G_1 \mid G_2 \mid \cdots \mid G_i]$, has minimum distance d_i such that $d_i < d_j$ for all $1 \leqslant i < j \leqslant m$. The depth of the subcode $V_1^{(i)}$ is i, by definition. Note that the code $V_1^{(m)}$ is the same as the code V_1.

Such a code can be incorporated into a GH-ARQ scheme as follows. Let I denote a block which is formed based on the message D and the (n,k) code V_0. The mn-bit long codeword is formed using I and the (mn,n) code V_1. Let such a codeword be represented by $\underline{c}^T = (\underline{c}_1^T \ \underline{c}_2^T \ \cdots \ \underline{c}_m^T)$, where the vector $\underline{c}_i$ corresponds to G_i, $i = 1,2,\ldots, m$ and has length n. We know that the data block I can be recovered uniquely from the knowledge of $\underline{c}_i$ if and only if the corresponding $(n \times n)$ matrix G_i is invertible. Therefore, the generator matrix G_1 is assumed to be invertible so that the data block can be computed from $\underline{c}_1$ alone (first transmission). In addition, it is desirable (although, not necessary) that the $(n \times n)$ matrices G_i, $i = 2,\ldots, m$ be invertible as well. This is particularly important for the case in which a burst of errors might destroy one of the transmissions, yet leave the other transmissions relatively error-free. New codes having these desired properties are discussed in the sequel.

For the block I to be transmitted, the sequence of blocks which are transmitted to the receiver, until the block is successfully accepted, is given by $\underline{c}_1, \underline{c}_2, \ldots, \underline{c}_m, \underline{c}_1, \ldots, \underline{c}_m, \underline{c}_1, \ldots$. Upon receiving a block, say $\underline{c}_i$, the receiver adopts one of the following two strategies:

(1) Invert $\underline{c}_i$ (if the associated G_i is invertible), perform error-detection based on V_0. If required, decode using $\underline{c}_i$ and the previously received blocks; perform error-detection (based on V_0) again, or

(2) Decode using $\underline{c}_i$ and the previously received blocks; perform error-detection based on V_0.

An ACK is sent to the transmitter whenever no errors are detected. For the above transmitted sequence of blocks, the receiver performs error-correction on the basis of the codes $V_1^{(2)}$, $V_1^{(3)}$, ..., V_1, V_1, ... having the distance $d_2, d_3, ..., d, d, ...$. Thus, with each retransmission, a code having a higher distance, that is, a larger error-correcting capability, is used for error-correction until we reach the code V_1.

Note that the type-II hybrid ARQ scheme described in Chapter 6 is a special case of the GH-ARQ presented here, for which the depth $m = 2$, the matrices G_1 and G_2 are invertible and, furthermore, the matrix G_1 is an identity matrix.

7.1.1 Complexity of the GH-ARQ scheme

We briefly analyse the complexity of the GH-ARQ scheme described above. To begin with, for any block I to be transmitted, the transmitter computes a codeword of length mn based on V_1. Therefore, a buffer of length mn bits is required at the transmitter and the receiver for each of the blocks to be transmitted. The transmitter also requires an encoder only for the code V_1. The receiver requires a decoder for each of the codes $V_1^{(2)}, ..., V_1^{(m-1)}$, V_1. Also, an inverter circuit is needed for each of the $\underline{c}_i$, $i = 1, 2, ..., m$.

From the analysis of the system complexity given here, the complexity of implementing the GH-ARQ scheme may appear to be prohibitive.

Specifically, the configuration of the receiver seems very complex as it

requires decoders for more than one code, namely $V_1^{(2)}, \ldots, V_1^{(m-1)}, V_1$,

and if the decoding procedure for these codes is not the same, the cost

of having (m-1) decoder circuits at the receiver may offset any gain in

system performance. Alternatively, if the decoder configuration for the

codes is the same, then the GH-ARQ scheme may offer a significant advan-

tage over the type-II ARQ systems while keeping the additional system

complexity to as low as possible.

A class of linear codes having the necessary properties was

discussed in Chapters 4 and 5. These codes are referred to as the KM

(Krishna-Morgera) codes in the sequel. The decoder configuration for

the KM codes, given in Figure 5.1, can alternatively be described as a

procedure which computes a small number of candidate information

polynomials and selects that candidate information polynomial as the

transmitted information polynomial whose corresponding codevector

differs from the received vector in the least number of places.

Therefore, the decoder configuration can also be described by the block

diagram shown in Figure 7.1.

Since the (12,4,5) KM code will be referred to extensively in this

chapter, the generator matrix of this code is reproduced in the

following. The generator matrix has 4 blocks corresponding to the

computation $Z_i(u)Y_i(u)$ modulo $P_i(u)$, i=1,2,3, where $P_1(u) = u^2$, $P_2(u) =$

(u^2+1) and $P_3(u) = (u^2+u+1)$, and the computation of the wraparound for

s = 2. It is given by,

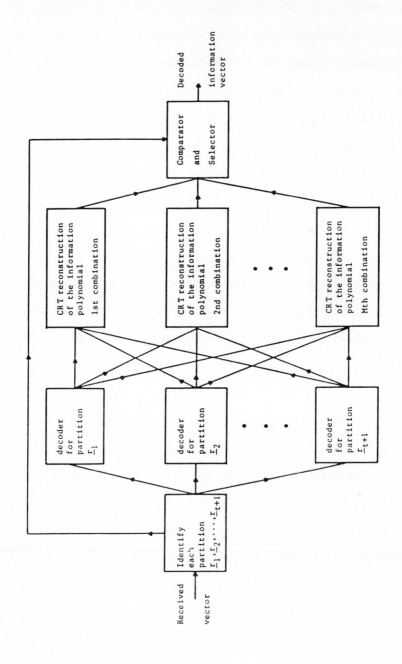

Figure 7.1. Block diagram for the decoder configuration of KM codes

$$C = \begin{bmatrix} 1 & 0 & 1 & 1 & 0 & 1 & 1 & 1 & 0 & 0 & 0 & 0 \\ 0 & 1 & 1 & 0 & 1 & 1 & 0 & 1 & 1 & 0 & 0 & 0 \\ 0 & 0 & 0 & 1 & 0 & 1 & 1 & 0 & 1 & 0 & 1 & 1 \\ 0 & 0 & 0 & 0 & 1 & 1 & 1 & 1 & 0 & 1 & 0 & 1 \end{bmatrix} \qquad (7.2)$$

It has been stated earlier that the actual minimum distance of the above code is 6. Before proceeding further, we outline the basic procedure to obtain the partitions of the KM codes required in the application of these codes to the GH-ARQ scheme.

7.2 Procedure for Partitioning the Generator Matrix of KM Codes

Consider an (n,k) KM code. The generator matrix C of the code has $(t+1)$ blocks, where each block C_i corresponds to a computation of the type,

$$\Phi_i(u) \equiv Z_i(u)Y_i(u) \quad \text{modulo } P_i(u).$$

If $\deg[P_i(u)] = \alpha_i$, then there are exactly α_i $\ell.i.$ columns in C_i corresponding to the reduction of $Z(u)$ modulo $P_i(u)$ to obtain,

$$Z_i(u) \equiv Z(u) \quad \text{modulo } P_i(u).$$

As each of α_i is small, the above computation for $\Phi_i(u)$ can be performed such that the rank of the remaining $n_i - \alpha_i$ columns is the maximum of α_i and $n_i - \alpha_i$. This is to ensure that the partitions of the generator matrix are invertible. Also, since the information polynomial is of degree $k-1$, it can be computed from any set of k $\ell.i.$ residues. Furthermore, the block C_i corresponds to the computation

$$\Phi_i(u) \equiv Z_i(u)Y_i(u) \quad \text{modulo } (u+a_i)^{\alpha_i}$$

where $a_i \in GF(2)$, can be partitioned into subblocks C_i^1, $C_i^2, \ldots, C_i^{\alpha_i}$ such that subblock C_i^1 corresponds to the computation

$$\Phi_i(u) \equiv Z_i(u)Y_i(u) \quad \text{modulo } (u+a_i)$$

and, in general, the subblocks $(C_i^1 \ C_i^2 \cdots C_i^j)$ correspond to the computation

$$\Phi_i(u) \equiv Z_i(u)Y_i(u) \quad \text{modulo } (u+a_i)^j$$

$$\text{for } j = 1, 2, \ldots, \alpha_i.$$

This property also holds for the wraparound block. Thus, the minimum distance of the code is increased by simply introducing columns to the generator matix. Also, these columns are chosen to be $\ell.i.$ so that the associated partitions are invertible.

Example. Consider the generator matrix of the (12,4,5) KM code given in (7.2). The block corresponding to the computation $Z_1(u)Y_1(u)$ modulo u^2 is given by,

$$C_1 = \begin{bmatrix} 1 & 0 & 1 \\ 0 & 1 & 1 \\ 0 & 0 & 0 \\ 0 & 0 & 0 \end{bmatrix}$$

This block can be partitioned into two subblocks C_1^1 and C_1^2, where

$$C_1^1 = \begin{bmatrix} 1 \\ 0 \\ 0 \\ 0 \end{bmatrix}$$

and $\quad C_1^2 = \begin{bmatrix} 0 & 1 \\ 1 & 1 \\ 0 & 0 \\ 0 & 0 \end{bmatrix}$

such that C_1^1 corresponds to the computation $Z_1(u)Y_1(u)$ modulo u. Similarly the block C_2 corresponding to the computation $Z_2(u)Y_2(u)$ modulo (u^2+1) is given by,

$$C_2 = \begin{bmatrix} 1 & 0 & 1 \\ 0 & 1 & 1 \\ 1 & 0 & 1 \\ 0 & 1 & 1 \end{bmatrix}$$

This block can be partitioned into two subblocks C_2^1 and C_2^2, where

$$C_2^1 = \begin{bmatrix} 1 \\ 1 \\ 1 \\ 1 \end{bmatrix}$$

$$C_2^2 = \begin{bmatrix} 1 & 0 \\ 0 & 1 \\ 1 & 0 \\ 0 & 1 \end{bmatrix}$$

and C_2^1 corresponds to the computation $Z_2(u)Y_2(u)$ modulo $(u+1)$. Finally, the wraparound block C_4 for $s = 2$ is given by,

$$C_4 = \begin{bmatrix} 0 & 0 & 0 \\ 0 & 0 & 0 \\ 0 & 1 & 1 \\ 1 & 0 & 1 \end{bmatrix}$$

This block can be partitioned into subblocks C_4^1 and C_4^2, where

$$C_4^1 = \begin{bmatrix} 0 \\ 0 \\ 0 \\ 1 \end{bmatrix}$$

$$C_4^2 = \begin{bmatrix} 0 & 0 \\ 0 & 0 \\ 1 & 1 \\ 0 & 1 \end{bmatrix}$$

and C_4^1 corresponds to the wraparound computation for $s = 1$.

The $(12,4,5)$ code is obtained from the computation $\Phi(u) = Z(u)Y(u)$, where $P(u) = u^2(u^2+1)(u^2+u+1)$ and $s = 2$. Consequently, if the subblocks C_1^2 and C_4^2 are deleted from the generator matrix of the $(12,4,5)$ code, the resulting code is a $(8,4,3)$ code corresponding to the computation $\Phi(u) = Z(u)Y(u)$, where $Z(u) = z_0+z_1u+z_2u^2+z_3u^3$, $Y(u) = y_0+y_1u+y_2u^2$, $P(u) = u(u^2+1)(u^2+u+1)$ and $s = 1$. The generator matrix of the $(8,4,3)$ code can be divided into two partitions so that each of these partitions are invertible. Such an arrangement of the columns results in the following form for the generator matrix of the $(12,4,5)$ KM code,

$$C = \left[\begin{array}{cccc|cccc|cccc} 1 & 1 & 0 & 1 & 1 & 1 & 0 & 0 & 0 & 1 & 0 & 0 \\ 0 & 0 & 1 & 0 & 1 & 1 & 1 & 0 & 1 & 1 & 0 & 0 \\ 0 & 1 & 0 & 1 & 1 & 0 & 1 & 0 & 0 & 0 & 1 & 1 \\ 0 & 0 & 1 & 1 & 1 & 1 & 0 & 1 & 0 & 0 & 0 & 1 \end{array} \right] \tag{7.3}$$

$$= \left[C_1 \mid C_2 \mid C_3 \right] .$$

It is easy to verify that the matrices C_1, C_2 and C_3 are <u>invertible</u> and the matrix $\left[C_1 \mid C_2 \right]$ is the generator matrix of the $(8,4,3)$ KM code.

7.3   A GH-ARQ Scheme Based on KM Codes

We now describe a GH-ARQ scheme that employs KM codes for error-correction. To be specific, we take the example of the (12,4,5) KM code and illustrate the complete scheme for such a code. Such a scheme, however, is general in nature, and in Appendix D we present the generator matrix of several KM codes along with their useful features for such an application.

Let us assume that we wish to use the above code in the GH-ARQ system. Choosing an (n,k) code V_0, for error-detection, we proceed as follows. Define three matrices G_1, G_2 and G_3 each of dimension (n×n) as,

$$G_i = C_i \otimes I_{n/4} \qquad i = 1,2,3 \qquad\qquad (7.4)$$

where $I_{n/4}$ is an identity matrix of order n/4 and $\otimes$ represents the Kronecker product of two matrices [33]. It is worthwhile to note here that since C_i, i = 1,2,3 is invertible, the matrix G_i, i = 1,2,3 is also invertible and G_i^{-1} is given by,

$$G_i^{-1} = C_i^{-1} \otimes I_{n/4} \qquad i = 1,2,3.$$

Let $\underline{\ell}$ denote the vector corresponding to the block I to be transmitted. The transmitter computes three (n×1) vectors,

$$\underline{c}_i^T = \underline{\ell}^T G_i \qquad\qquad i = 1,2,3.$$

Since G_i, i = 1,2,3 is invertible, the data block I can be computed uniquely from $\underline{c}_i$, i = 1,2,3. Note that the above encoding procedure corresponds to partitioning the block $\underline{\ell}$ into subblocks of length 4 each, and then encoding each of these subblocks using the (12,4,5) KM code. Let I_1, I_2 and I_3 denote the blocks associated with the vectors $\underline{c}_1$, $\underline{c}_2$, and $\underline{c}_3$, respectively. The transmission procedure for the block I is shown in Figure 7.2.

114

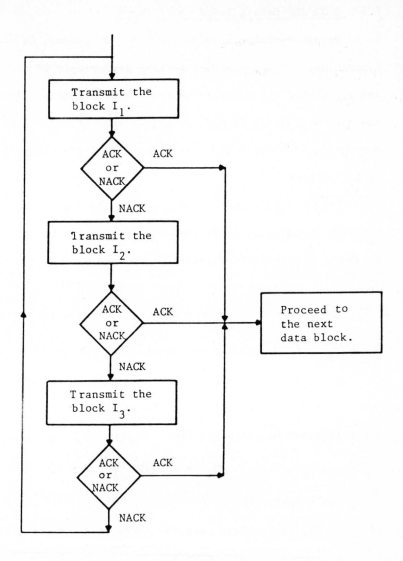

Figure 7.2. Transmission procedure for a GH–ARQ scheme
using depth 3 code for error-correction

Let $\tilde{I}_i$ denote the received block corresponding to the block I_i and $\hat{I}_i$ be an estimate of the block I based on $\tilde{I}_i$ and the matrix G_i, $i = 1,2,3$. If no errors have taken place during transmission, then $\tilde{I}_i = I_i$ and consequently $\hat{I}_i = I$, $i = 1,2,3$. The receiver configuration for the block I is given in Figure 7.3. In Figure 7.3, the integers i and j correspond to the total number of transmissions for the block I and the most recently received block, respectively.

It was implicitly assumed above that the length of the block I was an integral multiple of 4, the dimension of the KM code used. In general, the length of a block in an ARQ scheme may be restricted due to other system constraints. Keeping this in mind, we present a number of KM codes in Appendix D that can be used in the GH-ARQ scheme for adaptive error control. The generator matrices (in block form) and the important properties of such codes are also given.

7.4 Error-Detection

In this section, we analyse the error-detection capability of the GH-ARQ technique. This is an important parameter for the performance of the system. Let P_e denote the probability of an undetected error of the (n,k) error-detection code V_0. If V_0 is properly chosen, P_e is upperbounded by,

$$P_e \leq [1 - (1 - \varepsilon)^k] \, 2^{-(n-k)} \qquad 0 \leq \varepsilon \leq \tfrac{1}{2} \qquad (7.5)$$

where ε is the bit error rate of the channel [32]. If a code that satisfies the above bound is used for ARQ systems, then P_e can be made very small by using a large number of parity bits. The bound is an existence bound and very few codes have been theoretically shown to satisfy it [34]. However, it is intuitively seen that there is an abundance of codes that will satisfy the bound. We note that the

116

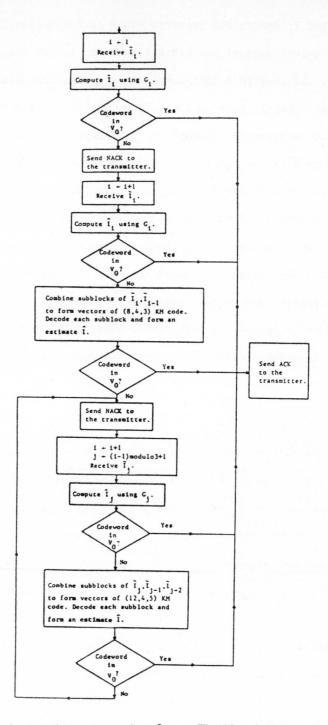

Figure 7.3. Receiver operation for a GH-ARQ scheme using
(12,4,5) KM code for error-correction

reliability of an ARQ scheme depends strongly on the existence of codes for which P_e can be made arbitrarily small. In the following, we examine the probability of undetected error for each transmission in a GH-ARQ system as compared to the probability of undetected error for each transmission in an ARQ scheme using the code V_0.

Let $\underline{r}$ denote the received vector and the $(n-k) \times n$ matrix H be the parity-check matrix of the code V_0. The procedure for error-detection corresponds to computing the vector-matrix product $\underline{r}^T H^T$. If the product results in the zero vector, the vector $\underline{r}$ is a codeword in V_0 and is declared error-free. In the GH-ARQ system, the receiver first takes the inverse of the received vector $\underline{r}$ in order to obtain an estimate of the codeword I and then examines it using V_0. Such a procedure can be described mathematically as the vector-matrix product $\underline{r}^T G_i^{-1} H^T$, where the subscript i represents the ith transmission. Let $\widetilde{H}_i^T = G_i^{-1} H^T$; we can, equivalently, state that, in a GH-ARQ system, an error pattern $\underline{e}$ in the ith transmission of a block will be undetectable iff $\underline{e}$ is a codeword in the linear code having $\widetilde{H}_i$ as its parity-check matrix.

Though it is not possible to show at this stage that the probability of undetected error in the GH-ARQ scheme satisfies the bound given in (7.5), we present two examples which satisfy the bound.

Example 1. Let V_0 be the (500,480) code obtained by shortening the distance 5 (1023,1003) BCH code and V_1 be the (12,4,5) KM code described in Section 7.2. Figure 7.4 shows the probability of undetected error when V_0 is used for error-detection in a GH-ARQ scheme that uses the (12,4,5) code for error-correction. Note that, in this case, there are

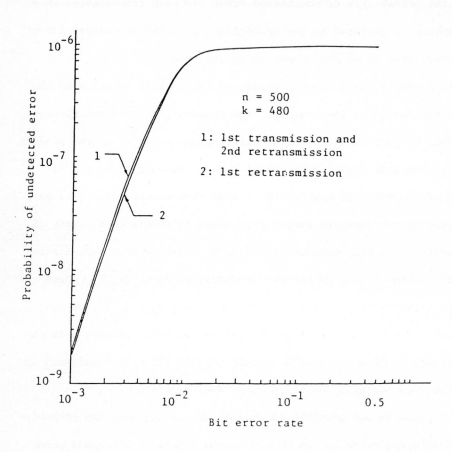

Figure 7.4. Probability of undetected error for the GH-ARQ scheme using (12,4,5) KM code for error-correction

3 plots for the probability of undetected error corresponding to the
first transmission and first and second retransmissions.

Example 2. For the same code V_0 as in Example 1, Figure 7.5 shows the
probability of undetected error for successive transmissions in a GH-ARQ
scheme that uses (15,5,5) KM code of Appendix D for adaptive
error-correction.

We observe that in both cases, the probability of undetected error
is a monotonic function of ε, $0 \leqslant \varepsilon \leqslant \frac{1}{2}$, a condition necessary and sufficient for a code to satisfy the bound of (7.5) [34].

7.4.1 Burst error-detection capability of GH-ARQ scheme

Usually, for ARQ applications, the error-detection code V_0 is
chosen as an (n,k) cyclic code due to its burst error-detection
capability. Every (n,k) cyclic code can detect any burst of length
(n-k) or less as no codeword of a (n,k) cyclic code is a burst of length
(n-k) or less [9]. A natural question to consider is the burst error-
detection capability of the codes used in the GH-ARQ scheme. For the
GH-ARQ scheme, the receiver multiplies subblocks of the received vector
with the inversion matrix, i.e., C_i^{-1}. Therefore, if there are errors in
a subblock, these errors are contained within the subblock itself after
the inversion. For the worst case, we assume that if there is an error
in a subblock, all the digits in the subblock are in error after inversion. If ℓ' is the length of each subblock, and n' is the number of
subblocks that are affected by a burst of errors, then, after inversion,
the length of the burst is at most $\ell'n'$. For a burst to be detectable,
we have $\ell'n' \leqslant (n-k)$, or, $n' \leqslant \text{Int}[(n-k)/\ell']$, where $\text{Int}[x]$ is defined as
the integral part of x. Therefore, the maximum value of n' is given by

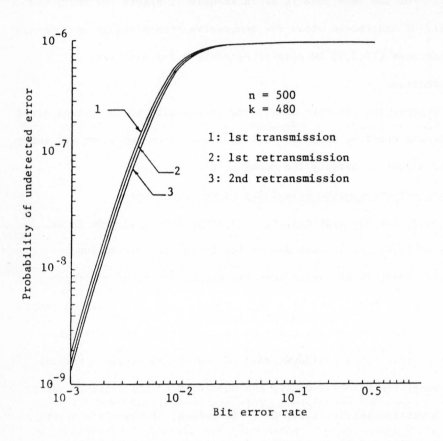

Figure 7.5. Probability of undetected error for the
GH-ARQ scheme using (15,5,5) KM code
for error-correction

$n'_{max} = Int[(n-k)/\ell']$. It is a simple exercise to establish that the

maximum length of a burst that affects only n'_{max} number of subblocks, is

$\ell'(n'_{max}-1) + 1$. Hence, the burst error-detection capability is under-

bounded by $\ell'(n_{max}-1) + 1$. For example, if $(n-k) = 20$, and $\ell' = 4$ (as

is the case for the $(12,4,5)$ code), then $n'_{max} = 5$ and the burst

error-detection capability is at least 17.

7.5 Performance Analysis of GH-ARQ Scheme

In this section, we analyse the throughput and reliability of a

GH-ARQ scheme. These are two important parameters associated with the

performance of any ARQ scheme.

7.5.1 Throughput

Since selective-repeat ARQ is the most efficient ARQ scheme, we

consider the throughput of the GH-ARQ scheme in the selective-repeat

mode. The throughput of such a scheme depends on the buffer size, and

in this regard, we restrict our attention to the infinite receive buffer

case. Also, it is assumed that the feedback channel is noiseless.

Let A_0^c, A_0^d, and A_0^e denote the events that a data block contains

no errors, detectable errors, and undetectable error, respectively, in

its first transmission. Similarly let B_i^c, B_i^d, and B_i^e denote the events

that the ith retransmission for a block contains no error, detectable

errors, and undetectable errors, respectively, $i \geqslant 1$. Note that the

ith retransmission corresponds to a total of i+1 transmissions for a

block. Also, upon the ith retransmission, let Q_i^c, Q_i^d, and Q_i^e be the

events that the block obtained by decoding the blocks received upto the

ith retransmission, contains no errors, detectable errors, and

undetectable errors, respectively. Finally, upon the ith

retransmission, let E_i^c be the event that receiver recovers the data

block, correctly; E_i^d be the event that the receiver cannot recover the

data block, detects the presence of errors, and requests the next

retransmission ; and E_i^e be the event that the receiver accepts an

erroneaous block. Therefore, using elementary law of probability,

$$E_i^c = B_i^c \cup B_i^d Q_i^c$$

$$E_i^d = B_i^d Q_i^d$$

$$E_i^e = B_i^e \cup B_i^d Q_i^e$$

where $B_i^d Q_i^c$, for example, denotes the intersection of the events B_i^d and

Q_i^c.

If A denotes the number of transmissions required to recover a block

successfully in any ARQ scheme, then the expected value of A is,

$$E[A] = Pr[A_0^c + A_0^e] + 2Pr[A_0^d(E_1^c + E_1^e)] + \cdots$$

$$(7.6)$$

$$+ (i+1)Pr[A_0^d E_1^d \cdots E_{i-1}^d (E_i^c + E_i^d)] + \cdots$$

and the throughput efficiency of the ARQ system is given by,

$$\eta = \frac{1}{E[A]} \left(\frac{k}{n}\right).$$

Here k/n is the rate of the code V_0 used for error-detection. The

inequalities, $Pr[E_i^c] \gg Pr[E_i^d]$ and $Pr[A_0^c] \gg Pr[A_0^e]$, may generally be

used to obtain an excellent approximation to $E[A]$ of (7.6).

The expression for $E[A]$ given in (7.6) is a general expression for the

average number of transmissions in an ARQ system. However, it involves

the probability of joint events which are difficult to calculate. We,

therefore, adopt the following two approaches for our further analysis.

(a) Approach 1. Wang et al [32] obtained a lowerbound on the throughput of the type-II hybrid ARQ system by analysing the throughput of an ARQ system which performs error-correction at every odd retransmission and only error-detection of every even retransmission. Their expressions can be appropriately modified when an (8,4,3) KM code is used for error-correction. These expressions are given in Appendix E. Note that this code corresponds to the simplest form of a GH-ARQ system having $m = 2$ and is the same as the subblock approach of [30]. Figure 7.6 shows the throughput of such a system. It also shows the throughput of the type-II hybrid ARQ system for the error-correcting capability $t_1 = 5,10$, and 20 of the code V_1 [32]. It can be seen that the throughput of the GH-ARQ system decreases slowly as it approaches 0.5. Although an exact analysis appears to be complex, it can be argued that since the receiver performs error-detection as well as error-correction upon the first retransmission, the probability of further retransmissions is reduced significantly and, therefore, a higher throughput is achieved. Also, so long as the probability of error-correction upon the first retransmission is high, the throughput will stay close to 0.5.

(b) Approach 2. Let us consider a GH-ARQ system, denoted by S_m that use an (mn,n) code V_1 for error-correction. Also define a series of GH-ARQ systems S_j as the GH-ARQ systems that use the subcodes $V_1^{(j)}$ of V_1 for error-correction, $j = 1,2,\ldots, m$. We further assume that $d_\alpha < d_\beta$ if $\alpha < \beta$, where d_θ denotes the minimum distance of the subcode $V_1^{(\theta)}$. If $E_j[A]$ is the expected number of transmissions for the GH-ARQ system S_j defined above, then we have,

124

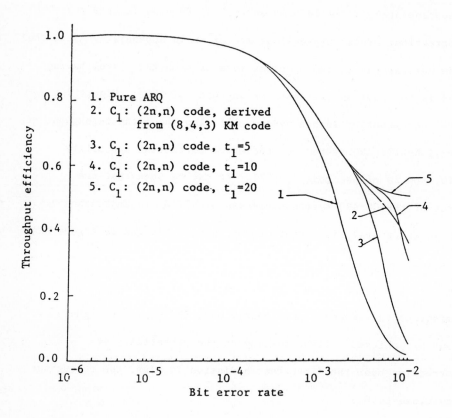

Figure 7.6(a). Throughput efficiency of the selective-
repeat GH-ARQ schemes using depth 2
codes for error-correction (n=500)

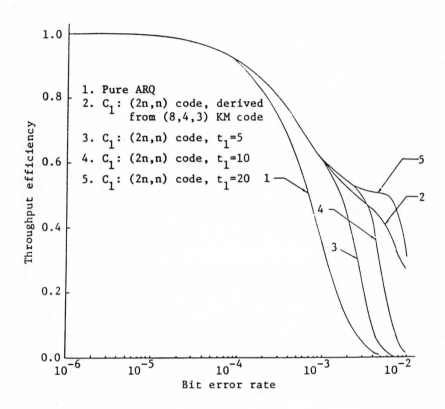

Figure 7.6(b). Throughput efficiency of the selective-
repeat GH-ARQ schemes using depth 2
codes for error-correction(n=1000)

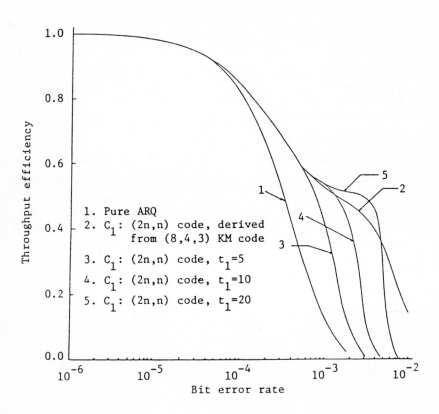

Figure 7.6(c). Throughput efficiency of the selective-
repeat GH-ARQ schemes using depth 2
codes for error-correction (n=2000)

$$E_j[A] = Pr_j[A_0^c + A_0^e] + \sum_{i=1}^{\infty} (i+1)Pr_j[F_i] \qquad j = 1,2,\ldots, m \qquad (7.7)$$

where $F_i = A_0^d E_1^d E_2^d \cdots E_{i-1}^d (E_i^c + E_i^e)$. Also, $P_{S_j}[i] = Pr_j[A_0^c + A_0^e]$

$+ \sum_{\ell=1}^{i-1} Pr_j[F_\ell]$ is the probability of the event that for GH-ARQ system S_j,

the receiver recovers the data block successfully in i transmissions.
Intuitively, we see that,

$$P_{S_\alpha}[i] = P_{S_\beta}[i] \qquad \text{for } i < \alpha \text{ and } i < \beta \qquad (7.8)$$

and $\qquad P_{S_\alpha}[i] > P_{S_\beta}[i] \qquad \text{for } \alpha > \beta \text{ and } i > \beta \qquad (7.9)$

Equations (7.8) and (7.9) are mathematical analogues of the statement:
'The probability of the event that a block is successfully accepted in i
transmissions is equal for two GH-ARQ schemes that use codes of depth α
and β for error-correction if $i < \alpha$ and $i < \beta$, since the two schemes
behave in an identically same manner for such a value of i. Conversely,
the probability of the event that a block is successfully accepted in i
transmissions is higher for a GH-ARQ scheme that uses a greater depth
code for error-correction.'

Therefore, the throughput of a GH-ARQ system using a depth α code
for error-correction is always higher than a GH-ARQ system that uses a
depth β code if $\alpha > \beta$. However, the relative improvement in the
throughput depends on the value of $P_{S_j}[i]$. For example, if the
error-rate of the channel $\varepsilon \to 0$, then, $P_{S_j}[1] = Pr_j(A_0^c) = (1-\varepsilon)^n \to 1$ and
$E_j[A] \to 1$ for $j = 1,2,\ldots, m$. Therefore, all the GH-ARQ schemes perform
equally well for low error rates. As ε increases, we require a larger
value of i, i.e., more transmissions for a data block in order to make

$P_{S_j}[i]$ close to 1, thereby, increasing $E_j[A]$. Also a GH-ARQ scheme $S_{\alpha+1}$ will perform significantly better than a GH-ARQ scheme S_α only if $P_{S_{\alpha+1}}[\alpha+1] \gg P_{S_\alpha}[\alpha+1]$ since $P_{S_{\alpha+1}}[\alpha] = P_{S_\alpha}[\alpha]$. Furthermore, for any GH-ARQ system, S_j, if $P_{S_j}[i] \rightarrow 1$ for the smallest value of i, then the throughput of such a system will fall atmost to 1/i. For example, for the type-II hybrid ARQ system (S_2), the throughput falls to 0.5 when retransmissions take place and ε is such that $P_{S_2}[2] \rightarrow 1$.

In Appendix E, we analyse the throughput of a GH-ARQ scheme using the (12,4,5) code by defining two systems inferior to the proposed system. The first inferior system A performs error-correction at every odd retransmission using the (8,4,3) code and only error-detection at every even retransmission. The second inferior system B performs error-correction at every third transmission using the (12,4,5) code and only error-detection for other transmissions. Since the expressions derived are similar to the expressions derived for Approach 1, only the pertinent details are given. The throughput of the actual GH-ARQ scheme is underbounded by the maximum of the throughputs of the two inferior systems. The expressions for the GH-ARQ schemes employing other codes for error-correction can also be derived using the expressions derived in Appendix E. Figures 7.7 and 7.8 show the throughput of GH-ARQ scheme using the (12,4,5) and (15,5,5) KM codes for error-correction for various values of data block length n. Such schemes have a depth of 3 and it is demonstrated in Figure 7.7 and 7.8 that the throughput of the scheme is close to 1/3 even for very high values of error ($\varepsilon \approx 10^{-2}$) and large block length (n = 2000).

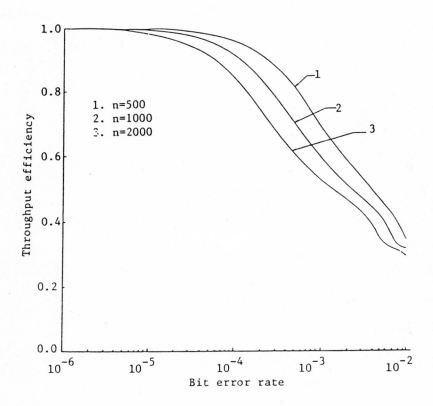

Figure 7.7. Throughput efficiency of the selective-
repeat GH-ARQ schemes using (12,4,5) KM
code for error-correction

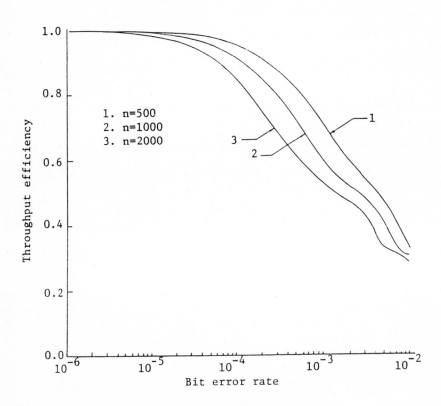

Figure 7.8. Throughput efficiency of the selective-
repeat GH-ARQ schemes using (15,5,5) KM
code for error-correction

7.5.2 Reliability

It has been established that the type–II hybrid ARQ system provides the same order of reliability as an ARQ system [32]. In the GH–ARQ scheme of depth m, error–detection is performed on the basis of codes having $\tilde{H}_i$, i=1,2,...,m as the parity check matrix. If P_{e_i} is the probability of undetected error for such codes, let

$$P_e = \max (P_{e_i}, i = 1,2,...,m).$$

Using similar arguments, it can be shown that the GH–ARQ system also provides the same order of reliability as an ARQ system using a code V_0 for error–detection having P_e as the probability of undetected error. This property is established in Appendix F. It is worthwhile to mention here that the P_{e_i}, i = 1,2,...,m are assumed to satisfy the bound given in (7.5), and therefore, P_e can be made arbitrarily small.

It is clear from the description of the ARQ schemes that these methods provide high system reliability, and are simpler to implement as compared to FEC schemes. However, at high channel error rates, the throughput of such systems falls rapidly while the throughput of a system using FEC is constant, irrespective of the channel conditions. In practice, ARQ and FEC schemes may be combined to provide high reliability as well as high throughput. If the channel characteristics are known a priori to be fairly constant, ARQ schemes can be combined directly with FEC schemes to provide high throughput. Such schemes are termed as type-I hybrid ARQ schemes.

In many system applications, the channel characteristics are not constant. Typical channels may be very quiet most of the time, but behave poorly during certain periods of time. Such channels are characterised by non-stationary error rates. One example of such a channel is the satellite channel. Thus the system is able to maintain high throughput during long periods without any error-correction, while, the performance deteriorates during poor channel behaviour. In such cases, the redundant information available upon successive tranmsissions is used to adaptively perform error-correction. These schemes are termed as type-II hybrid ARQ schemes.

In this part, the type-II hybrid ARQ schemes that are based on a $(2n,n)$ code are generalized to (mn,n) type-II hybrid ARQ schemes $(m \geqslant 2)$. These schemes are termed as GH-ARQ schemes. It is shown that the codes obtained in Part I, and referred to as KM codes in this part, can be incorporated into a GH-ARQ scheme to provide adaptively error-correction. These codes provide acceptable throughput even during extremely poor channel conditions (very high channel error rates). Since KM codes have small length and dimension, they are relatively less complex to implement as compared to codes having large length and dimension proposed elsewhere for similar applications. Another attractive feature of these codes is that the decoder configuration can be implemented using parallel architecture, making them an excellent candidate for high data rate communication systems. Finally, it is established that the GH-ARQ schemes described here also provide the same order of system reliability as a pure ARQ scheme.

CHAPTER 8

CONCLUSIONS

In Part I of this work, we have developed a new approach for obtaining linear codes. The properties of such codes depend on the computation of the aperiodic convolution of two sequences over the finite field of interest. The computation considered is bilinear in nature. The emphasis, in this work, is on algorithms over GF(2) and the associated binary codes, although codes over GF(3) are also discussed. A dense distribution of binary linear codes is available with a wide range of rate and distance properties. The length of the binary codes is determined by the complexity of the small polynomial multiplication algorithms involved and the overall length of the aperiodic convolution. Detailed examples of the code generation procedure are presented for convolution lengths of 6 and 16 over GF(2).

This hitherto unexplored approach to design of linear codes holds much promise for understanding structures of codes possessing good properties. We feel that this work offers means for unifying many good codes having disparate mathematical origins and encoding/decoding procedures.

The codes generated using the procedure given in this work may prove to be be extremely useful in system applications where codes of varying error-correcting capabilities are required to combat errors in a fluctuating noise environment. The problem can <u>alternatively</u> be considered as the problem of designing a linear code having a large dimension and distance by using the codes of small dimensions and distances as its building blocks.

The codes presented here can be generalised to codes over $GF(2^m)$. The length of the codes is <u>not restricted</u> to a maximum of (2^m-1) for such codes as is the case for the RS codes over $GF(2^m)$. It may be possible to find good linear codes over $GF(2^m)$ which, though weaker than the RS codes, may be relatively simpler to decode.

Due to their unique structure, the KM codes discovered in this work find an immediate application in ARQ systems for providing adaptive error-correction. It is clear from the description of the codes in Appendix D that it is possible to choose from a wide range of codes for error-correction in the generalized hybrid automatic repeat request system proposed here. These codes have a depth upto 4. We have demonstrated that these codes can be used to achieve high throughput under conditions when the channel is behaving rather poorly.

The emphasis in this work, is on GH-ARQ schemes which are simple to implement, and do not require excessive system overheads. The KM codes can be incorporated into a GH-ARQ system using simple encoding/decoding procedures. The length and the minimum distance of the KM codes can be varied easily without changing the encoder/decoder configuration, and, therefore, these codes are useful in providing adaptive error-control when frequent retransmissions are required due to degrading channel quality.

The proposed schemes compare well with the type-II hybrid ARQ scheme which is a special case of the general scheme described here. However, it may be relatively less complex to implement the codes which are described here as compared to implementing the large length BCH code described in [32] even for moderate error-correcting capability.

Since the codes studied here have small dimension, they can be decoded usign soft-decision decoding of block codes. This can lead to further improvement in the overall system performance. The receiver can also operate on a number of subblocks in parallel and the time duration of the complete procedure can be reduced. This feature may be important for high data rate applications.

Finally, we would like to state that all the GH-ARQ schemes proposed in this work are based on one class of codes and it may be possible to find other classes of codes which are equally simple in their encoding/decoding procedure and effective in providing higher throughput when the channel degrades.

8.1   Directions for Future Research

There are a number of distinct directions that a future researcher interested in this area can explore. Some of the important ones are as follows:

(1)   Study suitable architectures and implementation of the decoder configuration for the codes studied here, with special emphasis on high date rate applications.

(2)   Generalize the procedures to obtain efficient algorithms and the associated linear codes over $GF(2^m)$.

(3)   Study the complexity of the decoding procedure and the trade-offs between the complexity of the decoder and the length of the codes.

(4) Study the complexity of the decoding procedure in terms of soft-decision decodability of the codes.

(5) Investigate further into other potential applications for the KM codes. We feel that the unique properties associated with these codes may be further exploited to improve the performance and reduce the overall complexity of several communication systems.

We conclude this monograph by stating that all the binary codes generated in this work were found from the computation of a particular bilinear form and it may be possible to generate other classes of codes by considering different bilinear forms and their computation over the finite field of interest. We hope that this work will open up much fruitful and exciting research in this area.

REFERENCES

[1] R.E. Blahut, <u>Theory and practice of error control codes</u>, Addison-Wesley Publishing Company Inc., 1983.

[2] J.M. Pollard, "The fast Fourier transform in a finite field," <u>Math. of Computation</u>, Vol. 25, pp. 365-374, Apr. 1971.

[3] W.C. Gore, "Transmitting binary symbols with Reed-Solomon codes," <u>Proc. Princeton Conf. Inf., Sci., Syst.</u>, Princeton, pp. 495-497, 1973.

[4] R.T. Chien and D.M. Choy, "Algebraic generalisation of BCH-Goppa-Helgert codes," <u>IEEE Transactions on Information Theory</u>, Vol. IT-21, pp. 70-79, 1975.

[5] A. Lempel and S. Winograd, "A new approach to error-correcting codes," <u>IEEE Transactions on Information Theory</u>, Vol. IT-23, No. 4, pp. 503-508, July 1977.

[6] J. Justesen, "On the complexity of decoding Reed-Solomon codes," <u>IEEE Transactions on Information Theory,</u>, Vol. IT-22, pp. 237-238, 1976.

[7] D.V. Sarwate, "On the complexity of decoding Goppa codes, "<u>IEEE Transactions on Information Theory</u>, Vol.IT-23, pp. 515-516, 1977.

[8] S. Lin and D.J. Costello, Jr., <u>Error control coding: fundamentals and applications</u>, Prentice Hall 1983.

[9] W.W. Peterson and E.J. Weldon, Jr., <u>Error-correcting codes</u>, The MIT Press, 1978.

[10] F.J. MacWilliams and N.J.A. Sloane, <u>The theory of error-correcting codes</u>, North Holland Publishing Co., 1977.

[11] J.H. McClellan and C.M. Rader, <u>Number theory in digital signal processing</u>, Prentice Hall, 1979.

[12] H.J. Nussbaumer, Fast Fourier transforms and convolution algorithms, Springler-Verlag, 1981.

[13] H. Krishna and S.D. Morgera, "A computational complexity approach to the design of linear codes," International Symposium on Information Theory, Brighton, England, June 1985.

[14] H. Krishna and S.D. Morgera, "A computational complexity approach to the design of linear codes," submitted to Information and Control for publication.

[15] H. Krishna and S.D. Morgera, "A new error control scheme for hybrid ARQ systems," Presented at International Conference on Communications, Toronto, Canada, June 1986.

[16] R.W. Brockett and D. Dobkin, "On the optimal evaluation of a set of bilinear forms," Proceedings Fifth Annual ACM Symp. on Theory of Computing, pp. 88-95, 1973.

[17] A.V. Aho, J.E. Hopcroft and J.D. Ullman, The design and analysis of computer algorithms, Addison-Wesley Publishing Co., 1974.

[18] J. Hopcroft and J. Musinki, "Duality applied to the complexity of matrix multiplication and other bilinear forms," SIAM J. Computing, Vol. 2, pp. 159-173, Sept. 1973.

[19] J.L. Dornstetter, "On the computation of the product of two polynomials over a finite field," International Symposium on Information Theory, St. Jovite, Canada, Sept. 1983.

[20] H.J. Helgert and R.D. Stinaff, "Minimum distance bounds for binary linear codes," IEEE Transactiona on Information Theory, Vol. IT-19, No. 3, pp. 344-356, May 1973.

[21] M.D. Wagh and S.D. Morgera, "A new structured design method for convolutions over finite fields, Part I," IEEE Transactions on Information Theory, Vol. IT-29, No. 4, pp. 583-595, July 1983.

[22] G.C. Clark and J.B. Cain, Error-correction coding for digital communication, Plenum Press, 1981.

[23] S. Lin, D.J. Costello, Jr. and M.J. Miller, "Automatic-repeat-request error-control schemes, IEEE Communications Magazine, Vol. 22, No. 12 pp. 5-17, Dec. 1984.

[24] S. Lin and P.S. Yu, "A hybrid ARQ scheme with parity retransmission for error control of satellite channels," IEEE Transactions on Communications, Vol. COM-30, No. 7, pp. 1706-1719, July 1982.

[25] A.R.K. Sastry, "Improving automatic repeat request (ARQ) performance on satellite channels under high error rate conditions," IEEE Transactions on Communications, Vol. COM-23, pp. 436-439, April 1979.

[26] P.S. Yu and S. Lin, "An efficient selective repeat ARQ scheme for satellite channels and its throughput analysis, "IEEE Transactions on Communications, Vol. COM-29, No. 3, pp. 353-363, March 1981.

[27] E.Y. Rocher and R.L. Pickholtz, "An analysis of the effectiveness of hybrid transmission schemes," IBM Journal of Research and Development, pp. 426-433, July 1970.

[28] H. Krishna and S.D. Morgera, "A new error control scheme for hybrid ARQ systems," submitted to IEEE Transactions on Communications for publication.

[29] D.M. Mandelbaum, "Adaptive-feedback coding scheme using incremental redundancy," IEEE Transactions on Information Theory, Vol. IT-20, pp. 388-389, May 1974.

[30] J.J. Metzner, "Improvements in block-retransmission schemes," IEEE Transactions on Communciations, Vol. COM-27, pp. 525-532, Feb. 1979.

[31] J.J. Metzner and D. Chang, "Efficient selective repeat ARQ strategies for very noisy and fluctuating channels," IEEE Transactions on Communications, Vol. COM-33, No. 5, pp. 409-416, May 1985.

[32] Y.M. Wang and S. Lin, "A modified selective-repeat type-II hybrid ARQ system and its performance analysis," IEEE Transactions on Communications, Vol. COM-31, No. 5, pp. 593-607, May 1983.

[33] C.W. Therrian and K. Fukunaga, "Properties of separable covariance matrices and their associated Gaussian random processes," IEEE Transactions on Pattern Analysis and Machine Intelligence, Vol. PAMI-6, No. 5, Sept. 1984.

[34] T. Kasami, T. Klove and S. Lin, "Linear block codes for error detection," IEEE Transactions on Information Theory, Vol. IT-29, No. 1, Jan. 1983.

Noncommutative Algorithms for Small Degree Polynomial Multiplications

Algorithms B, and C are taken from [21] and Algorithm E is derived from Algorithm B by multidimensional techniques; Algorithms D and F are derived from Algorithms C and E by making suitable alterations. These algorithms are valid over any field.

<u>Algorithm A</u>   Degree 0, $z_0 \cdot y_0 = \phi_0$

Computation: direct 1 multiplication.

<u>Algorithm B</u>   Degree: 1, $(z_0 + z_1 u)(y_0 + y_1 u)$

$$= \phi_0 + \phi_1 u + \phi_2 u^2$$

Computation: 3 multiplications.

Let $m_0 = z_0 \cdot y_0$

$m_1 = z_1 \cdot y_1$

$m_2 = (z_0 + z_1) \cdot (y_0 + y_1)$,

then $\phi_0 = m_0$

$\phi_1 = -m_0 - m_1 + m_2$

$\phi_2 = m_1$

<u>Algorithm C</u>   Degree: 2, $(z_0 + z_1 u + z_2 u^2)(y_0 + y_1 u + y_2 u^2)$

$$= \phi_0 + \phi_1 u + \phi_2 u^2 + \phi_3 u^3 + \phi_4 u^4$$

Computation: 6 multiplications.

Let $m_0 = z_0 \cdot y_0$

$m_1 = z_1 \cdot y_1$

$m_2 = z_2 \cdot y_2$

$m_3 = (z_0 + z_1) \cdot (y_0 + y_1)$

$$m_4 = (z_1+z_2) \cdot (y_1+y_2)$$

$$m_5 = (z_0+z_2) \cdot (y_0+y_2),$$

then $\phi_0 = m_0$

$$\phi_1 = -m_0-m_1+m_3$$

$$\phi_2 = -m_0+m_1-m_2+m_5$$

$$\phi_3 = -m_1-m_2+m_4$$

$$\phi_4 = m_2.$$

Algorithm D Degree: 2, $(z_0+z_1u+z_2u^2)(y_0+y_1u+y_2u^2)$ modulo u^3

$$= \phi_0'+\phi_1'u+\phi_2'u^2$$

Computation: 5 multiplications.

Let $m_0 = z_0 \cdot y_0$

$$m_1 = z_1 \cdot y_1$$

$$m_2 = z_2 \cdot y_2$$

$$m_3 = (z_0+z_1) \cdot (y_0+y_1)$$

$$m_4 = (z_0+z_2) \cdot (y_0+y_2)$$

then $\phi_0' = m_0$

$$\phi_1' = -m_0-m_1+m_3$$

$$\phi_2' = -m_0+m_1-m_2+m_4$$

Algorithm E Degree: 3, $(z_0+z_1u+z_2u^2+z_3u^3)(y_0+y_1u+y_2u^2+y_3u^3)$

$$= \phi_0+\phi_1u+\cdots+\phi_6u^6$$

Computations: 9 multiplications.

Let $m_0 = z_0 \cdot y_0$

$m_1 = z_1 \cdot y_1$

$m_2 = (z_0 + z_1) \cdot (y_0 + y_1)$

$m_3 = z_2 \cdot y_2$

$m_4 = z_3 \cdot y_3$

$m_5 = (z_2 + z_3) \cdot (y_2 + y_3)$

$m_6 = (z_0 + z_2) \cdot (y_0 + y_2)$

$m_7 = (z_1 + z_3) \cdot (y_1 + y_3)$

$m_8 = (z_0 + z_1 + z_2 + z_3) \cdot (y_0 + y_1 + y_2 + y_3)$

then $\phi_0 = m_0$

$\phi_1 = -m_0 - m_1 + m_2$

$\phi_2 = -m_0 + m_1 - m_3 + m_6$

$\phi_3 = m_0 + m_1 - m_2 + m_3 + m_4 - m_5 - m_6 - m_7 + m_8$

$\phi_4 = -m_1 + m_3 - m_4 + m_7$

$\phi_5 = -m_3 - m_4 + m_5$

$\phi_6 = m_4.$

__Algorithm F__ Degree: 3, $(z_0 + z_1 u + z_2 u^2 + z_3 u^3)(y_0 + y_1 u + y_2 u^2 + y_3 u^3)$
modulo u^4

$$= \phi_0' + \phi_1' u + \phi_2' u^2 + \phi_3' u^3$$

Computation: 8 multiplications.

Let $m_0 = z_0 \cdot y_0$

$m_1 = z_1 \cdot y_1$

$m_2 = z_2 \cdot y_2$

$m_3 = z_3 \cdot y_3$

$m_4 = (z_0 + z_1) \cdot (y_0 + y_1)$

$m_5 = (z_0 + z_2) \cdot (y_0 + y_2)$

$$m_6 = (z_1 + z_2) \cdot (y_1 + y_2)$$

$$m_7 = (z_0 + z_3) \cdot (y_0 + y_3)$$

then $\phi_0' = m_0$

$$\phi_1' = -m_0 - m_1 + m_4$$

$$\phi_2' = -m_0 - m_2 + m_5$$

$$\phi_3' = -m_0 - m_1 - m_2 - m_3 + m_6 + m_7 .$$

Orthogonal Parity-Check Equations for Sufficiently Orthogonalisable

Codes

In this appendix, the orthogonal parity check equations on each of the error digits that correspond to the message digits are presented for the codes which are found to be sufficiently orthogonalisable. All the codes examined were 1-step sufficiently orthogonalisable with the exception of (24,6,9) code which was found to be 2-step sufficiently orthogonalisable.

(i)   The generator matrix of the (6,3,3) code in systematic form is given by,

$$C = \begin{bmatrix} 1 & 0 & 0 & 0 & 1 & 1 \\ 0 & 1 & 0 & 1 & 0 & 1 \\ 0 & 0 & 1 & 1 & 1 & 1 \end{bmatrix}$$

Let $(c_0 c_1 \cdots c_5)$ be the transmitted codevector and $(e_0 e_1 \cdots e_5)$ be the error vector. The 2 parity check sums orthogonal on e_0, e_1 and e_2 are $\{0+2+4,\ 0+3+5\}$, $\{1+2+3,\ 1+4+5\}$ and $\{2+0+4,\ 2+1+3\}$ respectively, where $\alpha+\beta+\gamma$ etc. corresponds to the parity check sum $e_\alpha + e_\beta + e_\gamma + \cdots$.

(ii) The generator matrix of the (8,4,3) code in the systematic form is given by,

$$C = \begin{bmatrix} 1 & 0 & 0 & 0 & 0 & 1 & 1 & 1 \\ 0 & 1 & 0 & 0 & 1 & 0 & 1 & 0 \\ 0 & 0 & 1 & 0 & 1 & 1 & 1 & 1 \\ 0 & 0 & 0 & 1 & 0 & 1 & 0 & 1 \end{bmatrix}$$

The 2 parity check sums orthogonal on e_0, e_1, e_2 and e_3 are

$\{0+2+3+5, \ 0+4+6\}$, $\{1+2+4, \ 1+3+6+7\}$, $\{2+0+3+5, \ 2+1+4\}$, and

$\{3+0+2+5, \ 3+1+6+7\}$ respectively.

(iii) The generator matrix of the $(10,5,3)$ code in the systematic

form is given by,

$$C = \begin{bmatrix} 1 & 0 & 0 & 0 & 0 & 0 & 0 & 0 & 1 & 1 \\ 0 & 1 & 0 & 0 & 0 & 1 & 0 & 0 & 1 & 1 \\ 0 & 0 & 1 & 0 & 0 & 1 & 0 & 1 & 0 & 1 \\ 0 & 0 & 0 & 1 & 0 & 0 & 1 & 1 & 1 & 0 \\ 0 & 0 & 0 & 0 & 1 & 0 & 1 & 0 & 1 & 1 \end{bmatrix}$$

The 2 parity check sums orthogonal on e_0, e_1, e_2, e_3 and e_4

are $\{0+1+3+4+8, \ 0+2+5+6+7+9\}$, $\{1+2+5, \ 1+0+3+4+8\}$ $\{2+1+5,$

$2+3+7\}$, $\{3+4+6, \ 3+2+7\}$ and $\{4+3+6, \ 4+0+1+2+9\}$ respectively.

(iv) The generator matrix of the $(10,3,5)$ code in the systematic

form is given by,

$$C = \begin{bmatrix} 1 & 0 & 0 & 0 & 0 & 1 & 1 & 1 & 0 & 1 \\ 0 & 1 & 0 & 1 & 0 & 1 & 1 & 1 & 1 & 0 \\ 0 & 0 & 1 & 1 & 1 & 1 & 0 & 0 & 1 & 1 \end{bmatrix}$$

The 4 parity check sum orthogonal on e_0, e_1 and e_2 are

$\{0+3+5, \ 0+1+6, \ 0+4+7+8, \ 0+2+9\}$, $\{1+2+3, \ 1+5+9, \ 1+0+6,$

$1+4+8\}$, and $\{2+1+3, \ 2+4, \ 2+5+6, \ 2+0+7+8\}$ respectively.

(v) The generator matrix of the $(12,6,3)$ code in systematic form

is given by,

$$C = \begin{bmatrix} 1 & 0 & 0 & 0 & 0 & 0 & 0 & 0 & 0 & 0 & 1 & 1 \\ 0 & 1 & 0 & 0 & 0 & 0 & 1 & 0 & 0 & 0 & 1 & 1 \\ 0 & 0 & 1 & 0 & 0 & 0 & 1 & 0 & 0 & 0 & 0 & 1 \\ 0 & 0 & 0 & 1 & 0 & 0 & 0 & 1 & 0 & 1 & 1 & 1 \\ 0 & 0 & 0 & 0 & 1 & 0 & 0 & 1 & 1 & 0 & 1 & 0 \\ 0 & 0 & 0 & 0 & 0 & 1 & 0 & 0 & 1 & 1 & 1 & 1 \end{bmatrix}$$

The 2 orthogonal parity check sums on e_0, $e_1, \ldots, e_5$ are

$\{0+1+3+4+5+10, \ 0+6+7+8+11\}$, $\{1+2+6, \ 1+3+4+5+10\}$, $\{2+1+6,$

$2+4+10+11\}$, $\{3+4+7,\ 3+5+9\}$, $\{4+3+7,\ 4+5+8\}$ and $\{5+4+8,$

$5+3+9\}$ respectively.

(vi) The generator matrix of the $(12,4,5)$ code in systematic form

is given by,

$$C = \begin{bmatrix} 1 & 0 & 0 & 0 & 0 & 0 & 0 & 1 & 0 & 1 & 1 & 1 \\ 0 & 1 & 0 & 0 & 0 & 1 & 1 & 0 & 0 & 1 & 1 & 1 \\ 0 & 0 & 1 & 0 & 1 & 0 & 1 & 1 & 1 & 0 & 1 & 0 \\ 0 & 0 & 0 & 1 & 1 & 1 & 0 & 0 & 1 & 0 & 1 & 1 \end{bmatrix}$$

The 4 orthogonal parity check sums on e_0, e_1, e_2 and e_3 are

$\{0+2+7,\ 0+1+9,\ 0+3+6+10,\ 0+5+11\}$, $\{1+3+5,\ 1+2+6,\ 1+0+9,$

$1+4+7+11\}$, $\{2+3+4,\ 2+1+6,\ 2+0+7,\ 2+10+11\}$, and $\{3+2+4,$

$3+1+5,\ 3+0+7+8,\ 3+9+11\}$ respectively.

(vii) The generator matrix of the $(14,3,7)$ code in systematic form

is given by,

$$C = \begin{bmatrix} 1 & 0 & 0 & 0 & 0 & 1 & 1 & 1 & 0 & 1 & 1 & 1 & 0 & 1 \\ 0 & 1 & 0 & 1 & 0 & 1 & 1 & 0 & 1 & 0 & 1 & 1 & 0 & 0 \\ 0 & 0 & 1 & 1 & 1 & 1 & 0 & 0 & 0 & 1 & 0 & 1 & 1 & 1 \end{bmatrix}$$

The 6 orthogonal parity check sums on e_0, e_1 and e_2 are

$\{0+6+8,\ 0+7,\ 0+2+9,\ 0+1+10,\ 0+3+11,\ 0+4+13\}$, $\{1+2+3,\ 1+5+9,$

$1+6+7,\ 1+8,\ 1+0+10,\ 1+11+13\}$, and $\{2+1+3,\ 2+4,\ 2+0+9,$

$2+6+11,\ 2+12,\ 2+7+13\}$ respectively.

(viii) The generator matrix of the $(14,5,5)$ code in systematic form

is given by,

$$C = \begin{bmatrix} 1 & 0 & 0 & 0 & 0 & 1 & 0 & 1 & 0 & 1 & 1 & 1 & 1 & 1 \\ 0 & 1 & 0 & 0 & 0 & 1 & 0 & 0 & 1 & 1 & 0 & 1 & 0 & 1 \\ 0 & 0 & 1 & 0 & 0 & 0 & 1 & 1 & 0 & 1 & 0 & 0 & 1 & 1 \\ 0 & 0 & 0 & 1 & 0 & 0 & 1 & 0 & 1 & 1 & 0 & 0 & 0 & 1 \\ 0 & 0 & 0 & 0 & 1 & 0 & 0 & 0 & 0 & 0 & 1 & 1 & 1 & 1 \end{bmatrix}$$

The 4 orthogonal parity check sums on e_0, $e_1,\ldots,e_4$ are

{0+1+5, 0+2+7, 0+4+10, 0+3+6+8+9}, {1+3+8, 1+0+5, 1+10+11,

1+2+4+6+7+13}, {2+3+6, 2+0+7, 2+10+12, 2+1+4+5+8+13},

{3+2+6, 3+1+8, 3+0+5+7+9, 3+10+11+12+13}, and {4+0+10,

4+5+11, 4+7+12, 4+9+13} respectively.

(ix)   The generator matrix of the (16,4,7) code in systematic form

is given by,

$$
C = \begin{bmatrix}
1 & 0 & 0 & 0 & 1 & 0 & 1 & 1 & 1 & 0 & 0 & 0 & 1 & 0 & 1 & 1 \\
0 & 1 & 0 & 0 & 1 & 1 & 0 & 0 & 1 & 1 & 1 & 0 & 1 & 1 & 1 & 0 \\
0 & 0 & 1 & 0 & 1 & 1 & 1 & 1 & 0 & 1 & 0 & 1 & 1 & 1 & 0 & 1 \\
0 & 0 & 0 & 1 & 1 & 0 & 1 & 0 & 1 & 1 & 1 & 0 & 0 & 1 & 0 & 1
\end{bmatrix}
$$

The 6 orthogonal parity check sums on e_0, e_1, e_2 and e_3 are

{0+4+9, 0+2+7, 0+1+14, 0+8+10, 0+5+12, 0+3+11+15}, {1+2+5,

1+0+14, 1+3+10, 1+4+6, 1+8+11+15, 1+7+12}, {2+11, 2+0+7,

2+1+5, 2+4+8, 2+12+14, 2+10+13}, and {3+1+10, 3+4+12, 3+6+7,

3+8+14, 3+5+9, 3+0+2+15} respectively.

(x)   The generator matrix of the (16,6,5) code in systematic form

is given by,

$$
C = \begin{bmatrix}
1 & 0 & 0 & 0 & 0 & 0 & 0 & 0 & 1 & 1 & 1 & 1 & 1 & 0 & 0 & 0 \\
0 & 1 & 0 & 0 & 0 & 0 & 1 & 1 & 0 & 0 & 0 & 0 & 1 & 0 & 1 & 1 \\
0 & 0 & 1 & 0 & 0 & 0 & 0 & 1 & 0 & 0 & 1 & 0 & 1 & 1 & 1 & 0 \\
0 & 0 & 0 & 1 & 0 & 0 & 1 & 0 & 1 & 1 & 1 & 0 & 0 & 1 & 0 & 1 \\
0 & 0 & 0 & 0 & 1 & 0 & 0 & 0 & 1 & 0 & 0 & 1 & 0 & 1 & 1 & 0 \\
0 & 0 & 0 & 0 & 0 & 1 & 0 & 0 & 1 & 1 & 0 & 1 & 1 & 1 & 0 & 1
\end{bmatrix}
$$

The 4 orthogonal parity check sums on e_0, e_1, ..., e_5 are

{0+2+8+13, 0+1+9+15, 0+7+10, 0+4+5+11}, {1+3+6, 1+2+7,

1+0+9+15, 1+5+8+11+13+14}, {2+1+7, 2+3+4+10+11+15, 2+6+9+12,

2+0+8+13}, {3+1+16, 3+8+11, 3+4+9+12+14, 3+2+5+7+15}, and

{4+8+9, 4+7+14, 4+0+5+11, 4+2+1+13+15} respectively.

(xi)   The generator matrix of the (18,5,7) code in systematic form

is given by,

$$C = \begin{bmatrix} 1 & 0 & 0 & 0 & 0 & 0 & 1 & 0 & 1 & 0 & 1 & 0 & 0 & 1 & 0 & 1 & 1 & 0 \\ 0 & 1 & 0 & 0 & 0 & 1 & 0 & 0 & 1 & 1 & 0 & 0 & 1 & 1 & 1 & 0 & 1 & 1 \\ 0 & 0 & 1 & 0 & 0 & 0 & 1 & 1 & 1 & 0 & 1 & 1 & 1 & 0 & 0 & 1 & 1 & 1 \\ 0 & 0 & 0 & 1 & 0 & 1 & 1 & 1 & 0 & 1 & 1 & 0 & 0 & 1 & 0 & 1 & 1 & 1 \\ 0 & 0 & 0 & 0 & 1 & 0 & 0 & 0 & 0 & 1 & 1 & 1 & 0 & 1 & 1 & 1 & 0 & 1 \end{bmatrix}$$

The 6 orthogonal parity check sums on e_0, e_1,...,e_4 are

$\{0+6+7,\ 0+8+12,\ 0+3+10+11,\ 0+9+13,\ 0+1+15+17,\ 0+2+5+16\}$,

$\{1+3+5,\ 1+7+9+11,\ 1+2+12,\ 1+4+14,\ 1+6+16,\ 1+0+15+17\}$,

$\{0+6+13+14,\ 2+3+7,\ 2+4+11,\ 2+1+12,\ 2+0+5+16,\ 2+9+17\}$,

$\{3+1+15,\ 3+2+7,\ 3+9+14,\ 3+0+11+15,\ 3+8+16,\ 3+4+12+17\}$ and

$\{4+5+9,\ 4+6+10,\ 4+2+11,\ 4+1+14,\ 4+0+7+15,\ 4+3+12+17\}$

respectively.

(xii) The generator matrix of (18,3,9) code in systematic form is

given by,

$$C = \begin{bmatrix} 1 & 0 & 0 & 1 & 1 & 1 & 0 & 1 & 1 & 0 & 1 & 1 & 0 & 1 & 1 & 1 & 0 & 1 \\ 0 & 1 & 0 & 1 & 1 & 0 & 1 & 0 & 1 & 0 & 1 & 0 & 1 & 0 & 1 & 1 & 0 & 0 \\ 0 & 0 & 1 & 0 & 1 & 0 & 1 & 1 & 1 & 1 & 0 & 0 & 1 & 1 & 1 & 0 & 1 & 1 \end{bmatrix}$$

The 8 parity check sums orthogonal on e_0, e_1 and e_2 are

$\{0+1+3,\ 0+4+6,\ 0+5,\ 0+2+7,\ 0+8+12,\ 0+11,\ 0+13+16,\ 0+9+17\}$,

$\{1+0+3,\ 1+4+7,\ 1+2+6,\ 1+8+13,\ 1+5+10,\ 1+12+16,\ 1+14+17,$

$1+11+15\}$ and $\{2+8+10,\ 2+0+7,\ 2+9,\ 2+1+12,\ 2+5+13,\ 2+14+15,$

$2+16,\ 2+11+17\}$ respectively.

(xiii) The genererator matrix of (20,4,9) code in systematic form

is given by

$$C = \begin{bmatrix} 1 & 0 & 0 & 0 & 0 & 1 & 0 & 1 & 0 & 1 & 0 & 0 & 1 & 0 & 1 & 1 & 1 & 1 & 0 & 1 \\ 0 & 1 & 0 & 0 & 1 & 1 & 0 & 1 & 0 & 1 & 0 & 1 & 0 & 1 & 1 & 0 & 0 & 1 & 1 & 0 \\ 0 & 0 & 1 & 0 & 1 & 1 & 1 & 1 & 1 & 0 & 0 & 1 & 1 & 1 & 0 & 1 & 1 & 1 & 0 & 0 \\ 0 & 0 & 0 & 1 & 0 & 0 & 1 & 1 & 0 & 1 & 1 & 1 & 0 & 0 & 1 & 1 & 1 & 0 & 1 & 1 \end{bmatrix}$$

The 8 parity check sums orthogonal on e_0, e_1, e_2 and e_3 are

$\{0+4+5,\ 0+7+11,\ 0+9+18,\ 0+2+12,\ 0+6+15,\ 0+8+10+16,\ 0+13+17,$

0+3+19}, {1+2+4, 1+5+10+16, 1+7+15, 1+6+11, 1+8+13, 1+14+19,

1+12+17, 1+3+18}, {2+3+6, 2+8, 2+0+12, 2+1+13, 2+7+9,

2+11+18, 2+15+19, 2+10+14+17}, and {3+2+16, 3+5+7, 3+8+9+17,

3+10, 3+4+11, 3+12+16, 3+1+18, 3+0+19} respectively.

(xiv) The generator matrix of (22,5,9) code in systematic form is given by,

$$C = \begin{bmatrix} 1 & 0 & 0 & 0 & 0 & 1 & 1 & 0 & 0 & 0 & 1 & 0 & 1 & 0 & 1 & 0 & 0 & 1 & 0 & 1 & 1 & 0 \\ 0 & 1 & 0 & 0 & 0 & 1 & 0 & 0 & 0 & 0 & 1 & 0 & 1 & 1 & 1 & 0 & 1 & 1 & 1 & 0 & 1 \\ 0 & 0 & 1 & 0 & 0 & 0 & 1 & 1 & 1 & 1 & 1 & 0 & 0 & 0 & 1 & 0 & 0 & 1 & 0 & 1 & 0 \\ 0 & 0 & 0 & 1 & 0 & 0 & 0 & 1 & 1 & 0 & 1 & 1 & 1 & 0 & 1 & 1 & 1 & 0 & 0 & 0 & 1 \\ 0 & 0 & 0 & 0 & 1 & 0 & 0 & 1 & 0 & 1 & 0 & 1 & 1 & 0 & 1 & 0 & 1 & 0 & 1 & 1 & 0 & 1 \end{bmatrix}$$

The 8 parity check sums orthogonal on e_0, $e_1,\ldots,e_4$ are

{0+2+8, 0+1+5, 0+8+10, 0+12+16, 0+13+17, 0+3+14+21,

0+7+15+19, 0+4+9+20}, {1+0+5, 1+3+13, 1+8+15, 1+9+18,

1+16+21, 1+11+12+20, 1+7+10+19, 1+2+4+6+14}, {2+0+6, 2+3+8,

2+4+9, 2+7+16, 2+11+21, 2+13+15, 2+1+5+14+18,

2+12+17+19+20}, {3+2+8, 3+1+13, 3+4+16, 3+7+9, 3+6+10,

3+11+18, 3+5+17, 3+0+14+21} and {4+2+9, 4+3+16, 4+7+8,

4+11+15, 4+5+14, 4+13+21, 4+0+1+18+20, 4+6+10+17+19}

respectively.

(xv) The generator matrix of (22,3,11) code in systematic form is given by,

$$C = \begin{bmatrix} 1 & 0 & 0 & 1 & 1 & 1 & 1 & 0 & 1 & 1 & 0 & 0 & 1 & 1 & 0 & 1 & 0 & 0 & 1 & 0 & 1 & 0 \\ 0 & 1 & 0 & 1 & 0 & 1 & 0 & 1 & 1 & 0 & 1 & 0 & 1 & 0 & 1 & 0 & 1 & 0 & 1 & 1 & 0 & 0 \\ 0 & 0 & 1 & 0 & 1 & 1 & 1 & 1 & 0 & 0 & 0 & 1 & 0 & 1 & 1 & 0 & 0 & 1 & 0 & 1 & 1 & 1 \end{bmatrix}$$

The 10 parity check sums orthogonal on e_0, e_1 and e_2 are

{0+1+3, 0+2+4, 0+5+7, 0+6+11, 0+8+10, 0+9, 0+12+16, 0+13+17,

0+15, 0+20+21}, {1+0+3, 1+4+5, 1+2+7, 1+8+9, 1+10, 1+12+15,

1+11+14, 1+16, 1+17+18+20, 1+19+21}, and {2+0+4, 2+3+5,

2+6+9, 2+7+10, 2+11, 2+13+15, 2+1+14, 2+17, 2+16+19, 2+21}

respectively.

(xvi) The generator matrix for (24,4,11) code in systematic form

is given by,

$$
C = \begin{bmatrix}
1 & 0 & 0 & 0 & 1 & 1 & 1 & 1 & 0 & 1 & 1 & 0 & 0 & 1 & 1 & 0 & 1 & 0 & 0 & 1 & 0 & 1 & 0 \\
0 & 1 & 0 & 0 & 0 & 0 & 1 & 0 & 1 & 1 & 0 & 1 & 0 & 0 & 1 & 1 & 0 & 1 & 1 & 1 & 0 & 0 & 0 & 1 \\
0 & 0 & 1 & 0 & 1 & 1 & 0 & 1 & 1 & 1 & 0 & 0 & 0 & 1 & 0 & 1 & 1 & 0 & 0 & 1 & 0 & 1 & 1 & 0 \\
0 & 0 & 0 & 1 & 0 & 0 & 0 & 1 & 1 & 0 & 1 & 1 & 1 & 0 & 0 & 1 & 1 & 1 & 0 & 1 & 1 & 1 & 0 & 1
\end{bmatrix}
$$

The 10 parity check sums orthogonal on e_0, e_1, e_2 and e_3 are

{0+2+4, 0+1+6, 0+3+10, 0+5+13, 0+7+16, 0+8+19, 0+11+23,

0+12+20, 0+14+18, 0+9+17+21}, {1+0+6, 1+2+9, 1+3+23, 1+18,

1+7+8, 1+11+20, 1+10+17, 1+19+21, 1+12+15+22, 1+5+13+14},

{2+0+4, 2+1+9, 2+3+16, 2+13, 2+7+10, 2+8+11, 2+12+21,

2+19+23, 2+15+17, 2+5+6+18}, and {3+0+10, 3+1+23, 3+2+16,

3+12, 3+4+7, 3+6+11, 3+13+21, 3+14+17, 3+9+19, 3+5+8+18}

respectively.

(xvii) The generator matrix for (26,5,11) code in systematic form

is given by,

$$
C = \begin{bmatrix}
1 & 0 & 0 & 0 & 0 & 1 & 1 & 0 & 1 & 1 & 0 & 1 & 1 & 1 & 0 & 0 & 0 & 0 & 1 & 1 & 1 & 0 & 1 & 1 & 0 & 1 \\
0 & 1 & 0 & 0 & 0 & 0 & 1 & 0 & 1 & 1 & 0 & 1 & 0 & 0 & 1 & 1 & 0 & 1 & 1 & 1 & 0 & 0 & 0 & 0 & 1 & 1 \\
0 & 0 & 1 & 0 & 0 & 1 & 0 & 0 & 1 & 0 & 1 & 0 & 1 & 0 & 1 & 0 & 1 & 1 & 1 & 0 & 0 & 1 & 1 & 1 & 0 & 1 \\
0 & 0 & 0 & 1 & 0 & 0 & 0 & 1 & 1 & 0 & 1 & 1 & 1 & 0 & 0 & 1 & 1 & 1 & 0 & 1 & 1 & 1 & 0 & 0 & 1 & 1 \\
0 & 0 & 0 & 0 & 1 & 0 & 0 & 1 & 0 & 1 & 1 & 0 & 1 & 1 & 1 & 1 & 0 & 1 & 1 & 1 & 0 & 0 & 0 & 1 & 0 & 1
\end{bmatrix}
$$

The 10 parity check sums orthogonal on e_0, e_1,...,e_4 are

{0+2+5, 0+1+6, 0+3+20, 0+17+25, 0+4+13, 0+10+12, 0+11+24,

0+14+18, 0+15+19, 0+7+8+9+22}, {1+0+6, 1+3+24, 1+12+25,

1+18+23, 1+11+20, 1+9+13, 1+7+15, 1+4+17+21, 1+10+19+22,

1+2+5+8+16}, {2+0+5, 2+3+16, 2+19+25, 2+13+23, 2+9+18,

2+15+17, 2+8+11, 2+7+10, 2+4+12+20, 2+1+21+24}, {3+0+20,

3+1+24, 3+2+16, 3+4+7, 3+6+11, 3+12+23, 3+14+17, 3+18+25,

3+5+10+13, 3+15+19+21+22}, and {4+0+13, 4+3+7, 4+8+25,

4+15+24, 4+22+23, 4+10+21, 4+11+19, 4+6+9, 4+1+16+17,

4+2+12+20} respectively.

(xviii) The generator matrix for (30,5,13) code in systematic form

is given by,

$$
C = \begin{bmatrix}
1 & 0 & 0 & 0 & 0 & 1 & 1 & 0 & 0 & 0 & 1 & 1 & 0 & 0 & 1 & 1 & 1 & 0 & 1 & 1 & 1 & 0 & 0 & 0 & 1 & 1 & 0 & 1 & 0 \\
0 & 1 & 0 & 0 & 0 & 1 & 0 & 1 & 0 & 1 & 1 & 1 & 0 & 1 & 1 & 1 & 0 & 0 & 0 & 1 & 0 & 0 & 1 & 0 & 1 & 0 & 1 & 1 & 0 & 0 \\
0 & 0 & 1 & 0 & 0 & 0 & 1 & 1 & 0 & 1 & 1 & 0 & 1 & 1 & 1 & 0 & 0 & 1 & 0 & 0 & 1 & 0 & 1 & 1 & 0 & 1 & 1 & 0 & 1 & 1 \\
0 & 0 & 0 & 1 & 0 & 0 & 0 & 0 & 1 & 1 & 0 & 1 & 1 & 1 & 1 & 0 & 0 & 1 & 0 & 1 & 1 & 1 & 0 & 1 & 1 & 1 & 0 & 0 & 0 \\
0 & 0 & 0 & 0 & 1 & 0 & 0 & 1 & 1 & 1 & 1 & 0 & 0 & 1 & 0 & 1 & 1 & 0 & 1 & 0 & 1 & 1 & 1 & 0 & 1 & 0 & 1 & 1 & 0
\end{bmatrix}
$$

The 12 parity check sums orthogonal on $e_0, e_1, \ldots, e_4$ are

{0+1+5, 0+2+6, 0+8+21, 0+18+29, 0+7+10, 0+9+14, 0+12+20,

0+13+26, 0+15+24, 0+4+16, 0+19+27, 0+11+22+25+28}, {1+0+6,

1+11+21, 1+20+26, 1+7+17, 1+12+13, 1+2+8+9, 1+3+24, 1+14+25,

1+6+10+23+29, 1+4+27, 1+16+19, 1+18+22+28}, {2+0+6, 2+7+27,

2+21+25, 2+3+12, 2+10+19, 2+15+26, 2+4+17, 2+13+24,

2+5+9+28, 2+29, 2+11+14, 2+8+16+20}, {3+4+8, 3+10+14,

3+16+21, 3+2+12, 3+5+15, 3+13+23+27, 3+1+24, 3+6+20,

3+17+18+28, 3+11+19, 3+7+9, 3+22+25+26+29}, and {4+3+8,

4+9+13, 4+11+15, 4+0+16, 4+16+26, 4+5+6+7, 4+2+27, 4+5+19,

4+23+29, 4+1+27, 4+20+25, 4+12+18+21} respectively.

(xix) The generator matrix of the (24,6,9) code in systematic form

is given by,

$$
C = \begin{bmatrix}
1 & 0 & 0 & 0 & 0 & 0 & 1 & 0 & 1 & 1 & 1 & 1 & 1 & 0 & 0 & 1 & 1 & 0 & 0 & 0 & 0 & 0 & 0 & 1 \\
0 & 1 & 0 & 0 & 0 & 0 & 1 & 0 & 1 & 0 & 1 & 1 & 0 & 1 & 1 & 0 & 1 & 1 & 0 & 0 & 1 & 0 & 1 & 1 \\
0 & 0 & 1 & 0 & 0 & 0 & 0 & 0 & 1 & 1 & 1 & 0 & 1 & 0 & 1 & 0 & 1 & 1 & 1 & 0 & 0 & 1 & 1 & 0 \\
0 & 0 & 0 & 1 & 0 & 0 & 0 & 0 & 1 & 1 & 0 & 1 & 1 & 1 & 0 & 0 & 1 & 1 & 1 & 0 & 1 & 1 & 0 & 0 \\
0 & 0 & 0 & 0 & 1 & 0 & 0 & 1 & 0 & 0 & 0 & 0 & 1 & 0 & 1 & 0 & 1 & 1 & 0 & 0 & 1 & 0 & 1 & 1 \\
0 & 0 & 0 & 0 & 0 & 1 & 0 & 0 & 0 & 0 & 1 & 0 & 0 & 1 & 0 & 1 & 1 & 0 & 1 & 1 & 1 & 0 & 1 & 1
\end{bmatrix}
$$

Let $E_1^1 = e_0 + e_1$, $E_2^1 = e_0 + e_2$, $E_3^1 = e_0 + e_3$, $E_4^1 = e_0 + e_5$, $E_5^1 =$

$e_0 + e_9$, $E_6^1 = e_0 + e_{11}$, $E_7^1 = e_0 + e_{12}$ and $E_8^1 = e_0 + e_{13}$ be eight selected sets of error digits. The 8 parity check sums orthogonal on E_1^1 are $\{4+5+13,\ 12+17,\ 3+11,\ 10+14+20,\ 9+13+18,\ 8+21,\ 6,\ 2+7+15+22\}$. Similarly, the 8 parity check sums orthogonal on E_2^1, E_3^1, E_4^1, E_5^1, E_6^1, E_7^1 and E_8^1 are $\{22+23,\ 16+20,\ 5+15+21,\ 3+4+12,\ 1+10+19,\ 9,\ 7+11+14,\ 6+13+18\}$, $\{20+23,\ 16+22,\ 5+15,\ 2+4+12,\ 1+11,\ 9+21,\ 8+13+18,\ 7+10+14+19\}$, $\{16+17,\ 3+15,\ 2+14+23,\ 4+11+20,\ 1+10+21,\ 9+18,\ 7+8+22,\ 6+13\}$, $\{2,\ 3+21,\ 5+18,\ 15+17+23,\ 14+19+20,\ 4+13+22,\ 8+11,\ 1+6+7+12\}$, $\{1+3,\ 4+5+20,\ 13+19,\ 12+18+23,\ 10+15+21,\ 8+9,\ 2+7+14,\ 6+16+22\}$, $\{4+21,\ 1+18+20,\ 5+13+17,\ 11+16+19,\ 10+23,\ 8+9+14,\ 2+7,\ 6+15+22\}$, and $\{4+23,\ 3+12+22,\ 11+19,\ 10+21,\ 1+9+18,\ 8+14+20,\ 2+7+16,\ 5+6\}$ respectively. From these orthogonal check sums, the sums E_1^1, $E_2^1, \ldots, E_8^1$ can be correctly estimated provided that there are no more than four errors in the error vector. Clearly, E_1^1, $E_2^1, \ldots, E_8^1$ are orthogonal on e_0. Hence, e_0 can be estimated from these sums. Furthermore, e_1, e_2, e_3, e_5, e_9, e_{11}, e_{12}, and e_{13} can be estimated from the above sums, once e_0 is estimated. Also, let $E_1^2 = e_4 + e_2$, $E_2^2 = e_4 + e_3$, $E_3^2 = e_4 + e_6$, $E_4^2 = e_4 + e_7$, $E_5^2 = e_4 + e_8$, $E_6^2 = e_4 + e_9$, $E_7^2 = e_4 + e_{10}$ and $E_8^2 = e_4 + e_{11}$ be another set of eight digits. The 8 parity check sums orthogonal on E_1^2, $E_2^2, \ldots,\ E_8^2$ are $\{1+14,\ 13+22,\ 0+3+12,\ 5+11+16,\ 8+9+17,\ 7+21,\ 6+18+23,\ 10+15+19+20\}$, $\{1+2+17,\ 13+20,\ 5+11+23,\ 0+10+22,\ 9+21,\ 8+16+19,\ 7,\ 6+14+15+18\}$, $\{5+23,\ 0+18+22,\ 2+16+19,\ 15+20,\ 1+12+21,\ 10+13+17,\ 9+14,\ 6+7+11\}$, $\{3+5+19,\ 0+16+19,\ 14+18+20,\ 11+12+17,\ 2+21,\ 1+8+9,$

6+13+15}, {3+18+23, 0+17, 5+16, 15+22, 1+12, 9+14+21,

7+10+19, 2+6+13+20}, {1+16+19, 2+13+23, 3+12, 11+17,

10+21+22, 5+8+20, 7+15+18, 6+14}, {2+3+23, 0+5+17, 16,

14+15, 12+13, 1+11+22, 9+20, 7+8+19}, and {0+5+20, 19+23,

16+18, 2+15+22, 10+13+14, 9+17, 6+7, 1+3+12+21}

respectively. From these orthogonal sums, E_1^2, E_2^2, ..., E_8^2 can

be correctly estimated provided that there are no more than

four errors in the error vector. We see that E_1^2, E_2^2, ..., E_8^2

are orthogonal on e_4. Therefore, e_4, and thereafter, e_2,

e_3, e_6, e_7 e_8, e_9, e_{10} and e_{11} can be estimated from these

sums.

Thus, using the above parity sum equations, e_0, e_1, ..., e_5

can be estimated correctly if no more than four errors are

present in the received vector. Hence, (24,6,9) code is a

2-step sufficiently orthogonalisable code.

Weight Distribution of Some Codes Obtained from the Aperiodic Convolution Algorithms

Code Parameters	0	7	8	9	10	11	12	13	14	15	16	17	18
(18,5,7)	1	5	6	6	6	5	3						
(20,6,7)	1	5	8	13	11	7	11	7	1				
(22,5,9)	1			4	7	8	3	4	5				
(24,6,9)	1			4	8	16	12	4	8	8	3		
(24,4,11)	1					2	6	4	2	1			
(26,7,9)	1				5	13	21	17	15	15	15	18	8
(26,5,11)	1					2	6	12	4	2	5		
(28,6,11)	1					4	8	16	12	4	7	8	4

Note: All blank entries are zeros.

List of KM Codes Suitable for GH-ARQ Schemes

In this appendix, we list several KM codes that can be used for adaptive error-control in a GH-ARQ scheme. Also, described are some of the properties that can be used to identify and generate these codes from the basic design procedure described in Chapters 4 and 5. Note that the generator matrices are completely characterised by the dimension k, design d, the choice of the polynomial P(u), and the wraparound s.

(15,5,5) KM Code. Here $P(u) = u^3(u^2+1)(u^2+u+1)$; $s = 2$. The generator matrix C is given by

$$C = \begin{bmatrix} 1 & 1 & 0 & 1 & 0 & 0 & 1 & 1 & 0 & 1 & 0 & 0 & 1 & 0 & 0 \\ 0 & 0 & 1 & 0 & 0 & 1 & 1 & 1 & 1 & 1 & 0 & 1 & 0 & 0 & 0 \\ 0 & 1 & 0 & 1 & 0 & 0 & 0 & 1 & 1 & 0 & 1 & 1 & 1 & 0 & 0 \\ 0 & 0 & 1 & 1 & 0 & 0 & 0 & 1 & 0 & 1 & 0 & 0 & 0 & 1 & 1 \\ 0 & 1 & 0 & 0 & 1 & 0 & 0 & 1 & 1 & 1 & 0 & 0 & 0 & 0 & 1 \end{bmatrix} \qquad (D\text{-}1)$$

$$= [C_1 \mid C_2 \mid C_3].$$

Features:

a. The matrices C_1, C_2, and C_3 are invertible.

b. $[C_1 \mid C_2]$ form the generator matrix of a (10,5,3) KM code corresponding to $P(u) = u^2(u^2+1)(u^2+u+1)$; $s = 1$.

No direct comparison of the above described code with the (15,5,7) BCH code [9] appears possible, since it is not known if the (15,5,7) BCH code satisfies the requirements to be useful for the application under consideration.

(18,6,6) KM Code. Here $P(u) = u^2(u^2+1)(u^2+u+1)(u^3+u^2+1)$; $s = 2$. The generator matrix C is given by

$$
C = \begin{bmatrix}
1\ 1\ 0\ 0\ 0\ 1 & 1\ 0\ 1\ 1\ 0\ 1 & 0\ 1\ 1\ 0\ 0\ 0 \\
0\ 0\ 1\ 1\ 0\ 0 & 1\ 0\ 1\ 0\ 1\ 1 & 1\ 1\ 0\ 1\ 0\ 0 \\
0\ 0\ 0\ 1\ 0\ 1 & 1\ 1\ 0\ 1\ 1\ 0 & 0\ 0\ 1\ 0\ 0\ 0 \\
0\ 1\ 0\ 1\ 0\ 1 & 1\ 1\ 1\ 0\ 0\ 1 & 0\ 0\ 0\ 1\ 0\ 0 \\
0\ 1\ 1\ 0\ 0\ 0 & 1\ 1\ 0\ 0\ 1\ 1 & 0\ 0\ 1\ 0\ 1\ 1 \\
0\ 1\ 1\ 1\ 1\ 1 & 1\ 0\ 0\ 1\ 1\ 0 & 0\ 0\ 0\ 1\ 0\ 1
\end{bmatrix}
$$

$$
= \begin{bmatrix} C_1 & C_2 & C_3 \end{bmatrix}
$$

(D-2)

Features:

a. The matrices C_1, C_2, and C_3 are invertible.

b. $\begin{bmatrix} C_1 & C_2 \end{bmatrix}$ form the generator matrix of a (12,6,3) KM code corresponding to $P(u) = u(u+1)(u^2+u+1)(u^3+u^2+1)$; $s = 1$.

(24,6,9) KM Code. If we append one more block, C_4, to the generator matrix of the (18,6,6) KM code of (D-2), we obtain the (24,6,9) KM code. Such a block corresponds to the computation for the factor polynomial (u^3+u+1) and is given by

$$C_4 = \begin{bmatrix} 1 & 0 & 0 & 1 & 0 & 1 \\ 0 & 1 & 0 & 1 & 1 & 0 \\ 0 & 0 & 1 & 0 & 1 & 1 \\ 1 & 1 & 0 & 0 & 1 & 1 \\ 0 & 1 & 1 & 1 & 0 & 1 \\ 1 & 1 & 1 & 0 & 0 & 0 \end{bmatrix}$$

Note that C_4 is not invertible.

(28,7,10) Extended KM Code[*]. Such a code is obtained by adding an overall parity to the (27,7,9) KM code having $P(u) =$ $u^2(u^2+1)(u^2+u+1)(u^3+u^2+1)(u^3+u+1)$ $s = 3$. The generator matrix C is given by

$$C = \left[\begin{array}{ccccccc|ccccccc|ccccccc|ccccccc} 1&1&1&1&0&0&0& 0&1&0&1&1&0&0& 0&1&1&0&0&0&0& 1&0&0&1&0&1&0 \\ 0&1&0&0&1&1&0& 1&1&0&1&0&0&0& 1&1&0&1&0&0&0& 0&1&0&1&1&0&0 \\ 0&1&1&0&0&1&0& 1&0&1&0&1&0&0& 0&0&1&0&0&0&0& 0&0&1&0&1&1&0 \\ 0&1&1&1&0&1&0& 0&1&1&1&0&0&0& 0&0&0&1&0&0&0& 1&1&0&0&1&1&0 \\ 0&1&0&1&1&0&0& 1&1&1&0&0&0&0& 0&0&1&0&1&1&1& 0&1&1&1&0&1&0 \\ 0&1&1&1&1&1&0& 1&0&0&0&1&1&1& 0&0&0&1&0&0&1& 1&1&1&0&0&0&0 \\ 0&1&1&0&1&0&1& 0&1&1&1&1&0&1& 0&0&1&0&0&1&0& 1&0&1&1&1&0&1 \end{array}\right] \quad (D-3)$$

$$= [C_1 \mid C_2 \mid C_3 \mid C_4]$$

Features:

a. The matrices C_1, C_2 and C_3 are invertible.

b. $[C_1 \mid C_2]$ form the generator matrix of a (14,7,3) KM code;
    $P(u) = u(u+1)(u^2+u+1)(u^3+u^2+1)$; $s = 2$.

---

*The decoder configuration of the extended KM code is the same as that of the associated KM code followed by a simple parity check.

c. $\begin{bmatrix} C_1 & \vdots & C_2 & \vdots & C_3 \end{bmatrix}$ form the generator matrix of a (21,7,6) KM code;

$P(u) = u^2(u^2+1)(u^2+u+1)(u^3+u^2+1)$; s = 3.

<u>(32,8,9) KM Code</u>. In this case, $P(u) = u^3(u^2+1)(u^2+u+1)$

$(u^3+u^2+1)(u^3+u+1)$; s = 3. The generator matrix C is given by

$$C = \begin{bmatrix}
1\ 1\ 0\ 0\ 1\ 0\ 0\ 0 & 1\ 1\ 1\ 0\ 1\ 1\ 0\ 0 & 0\ 1\ 0\ 0\ 0\ 1\ 0\ 0 & 0\ 0\ 1\ 1\ 0\ 1\ 1\ 0 \\
0\ 0\ 1\ 1\ 0\ 1\ 1\ 0 & 1\ 0\ 1\ 0\ 1\ 0\ 0\ 0 & 1\ 1\ 0\ 0\ 0\ 0\ 1\ 1 & 0\ 1\ 0\ 1\ 0\ 0\ 0\ 1 \\
0\ 1\ 0\ 1\ 0\ 0\ 1\ 0 & 1\ 1\ 0\ 1\ 0\ 1\ 0\ 0 & 0\ 0\ 0\ 0\ 0\ 0\ 0\ 1 & 1\ 1\ 1\ 0\ 1\ 1\ 0\ 0 \\
0\ 0\ 1\ 0\ 1\ 0\ 1\ 0 & 1\ 1\ 1\ 1\ 1\ 0\ 0\ 0 & 0\ 0\ 0\ 0\ 0\ 1\ 1\ 1 & 0\ 0\ 0\ 0\ 0\ 1\ 0\ 0 \\
0\ 1\ 0\ 1\ 1\ 1\ 0\ 0 & 1\ 0\ 1\ 1\ 0\ 0\ 0\ 0 & 0\ 0\ 0\ 0\ 0\ 0\ 1\ 0 & 0\ 0\ 0\ 1\ 1\ 1\ 1\ 1 \\
0\ 0\ 1\ 1\ 1\ 1\ 1\ 0 & 1\ 1\ 0\ 0\ 0\ 1\ 0\ 0 & 0\ 0\ 1\ 1\ 1\ 1\ 1\ 0 & 0\ 0\ 0\ 0\ 1\ 0\ 0\ 1 \\
0\ 1\ 0\ 0\ 0\ 1\ 0\ 0 & 1\ 1\ 1\ 1\ 1\ 1\ 1\ 1 & 0\ 0\ 0\ 1\ 0\ 1\ 0\ 1 & 0\ 0\ 0\ 1\ 1\ 0\ 0\ 0 \\
0\ 0\ 1\ 1\ 1\ 0\ 0\ 1 & 1\ 0\ 1\ 0\ 1\ 1\ 0\ 1 & 0\ 0\ 0\ 0\ 1\ 1\ 0\ 0 & 0\ 0\ 0\ 1\ 0\ 1\ 1\ 1
\end{bmatrix} \tag{D-4}$$

$= \begin{bmatrix} C_1 & \vdots & C_2 & \vdots & C_3 & \vdots & C_4 \end{bmatrix}$

Features:

a. The matrices C_1, C_2, C_3 and C_4 are invertible.

b. $\begin{bmatrix} C_1 & \vdots & C_2 \end{bmatrix}$ forms the generator matrix of a (16,8,3) KM code;

   $P(u) = u(u^2+1)(u^2+u+1)(u^3+u^2+1)$; s = 2.

c. $\begin{bmatrix} C_1 & \vdots & C_2 & \vdots & C_3 \end{bmatrix}$ forms the generator matrix of a (24,8,6) KM code;

   $P(u) = u^2(u^2+1)(u^2+u+1)(u^3+u^2+1)$; s = 3.

Note: The first 30 columns of the matrix given in (D-4) are the same as the (30,8,9) KM code. The last two columns are introduced in such a way as to render C_4 invertible and the overall length, n, a multiple of the dimension k.

APPENDIX E

Throughput Efficiency of GH-ARQ Schemes Using Depth 3 Code for

Error-Correction

In this appendix, expressions which can be used to compute the throughput of a GH-ARQ scheme using a depth $m=3$ code V_1 for adaptive error-correction, are presented. The generator matrix of V_1 has the form,

$$G = [G_1 \,|\, G_2 \,|\, G_3]$$

Let V_1 be derived from a $(3\ell', \ell')$ kM code having t_1 as its error-correcting capability, using (7.4). Also, Let $V_1^{(2)}$ be the code having $[G_1 \,|\, G_2]$ as its generator matrix. Clearly, $V_1^{(2)}$ is obtained from the $(2\ell', \ell')$ code having t_2 as its error-correcting capability. Note that $t_1 > t_2$.

In order to compute the throughput of the GH-ARQ system under consideration, we define two inferior GH-ARQ systems A and B. The first inferior system A performs error-correction at every odd retransmission using $V_1^{(2)}$ and error-detection at every even retransmission [32]. The second inferior system B performs error-correction at every third transmission using V_1 and only error-detection upon other transmissions. This approach is very similar to the approach in [32] and, therefore, only the pertinent details are given.

In the GH-ARQ scheme, error-detection is performed on the basis of the codes having $\tilde{H}_i$, $i = 1,2,3$ as the parity check matrix. If P_{e_i} is the probability of undetected error for such codes, let

$$P_e = \max (P_{e_i}, i = 1,2,3).$$

In the subsequent analysis, it is assumed that P_e satisfies the bound given in (7.5), and, therefore, can be made arbitrarily small. If P_c is the probability that the jth transmission of a block is received error free, then,

$$P_c = (1 - \varepsilon)^n.$$

Also, the probability that errors are detected in any transmission, is at least $1-P_c-P_e$. Since the analysis for the systems A and B is somewhat similar, we enclose the description for system B within parenthesis along with the description for the system A.

System A(B). For the two (three) consecutively received blocks $\tilde{I}_{i-1}$ and $\tilde{I}_i$ ($\tilde{I}_{i-2}$, $\tilde{I}_{i-1}$ and $\tilde{I}_i$) for a data block I, let,

q_0 = Probability of the event that correct decoding takes place based on $V_1^{(2)}$ (V_1).

y = Probability of the event that correct decoding takes place based on $V_1^{(2)}$ (V_1) and at least one of $\tilde{I}_{i-1}$ and $\tilde{I}_i$ ($\tilde{I}_{i-2}$, $\tilde{I}_{i-1}$ and $\tilde{I}_i$) is errorfree.

q_1 = Conditional probability of correct decoding based on $V_1^{(2)}$ (V_1), given that $\tilde{I}_{i-1}$ and $\tilde{I}_i$ ($\tilde{I}_{i-2}$, $\tilde{I}_{i-1}$ and $\tilde{I}_i$) are detected in error.

Therefore, probability of correctly obtaining I from $\tilde{I}_{i-1}$ and $\tilde{I}_i$ ($\tilde{I}_{i-2}$, $\tilde{I}_{i-1}$ and $\tilde{I}_i$) given that $\tilde{I}_{i-1}$ ($\tilde{I}_{i-2}$ and $\tilde{I}_{i-1}$) is detected in error, is given by,

$$P_t = P_c + (1 - P_c)q_1$$

For system A, $E[A]$ is underbounded by,

$$E[A]_A \leqslant \frac{2-P_c}{P_c+P_t-P_cP_t} \tag{E1}$$

The probabilities q_0, y and q_1 can be evaluated using the expressions,

$$q_0 = [\sum_{j=0}^{t_2} \binom{2\ell'}{j} \varepsilon^j (1-\varepsilon)^{2\ell'-j}]^{n/\ell'} \tag{E2}$$

$$y = (1-\varepsilon)^n \{2[\sum_{j=0}^{t_2} \binom{\ell'}{j} \varepsilon^j (1-\varepsilon)^{\ell'-j}]^{n/\ell'} - (1-\varepsilon)^n\} \tag{E3}$$

and $q_1 = \frac{1}{1-y}(q_0 - y)$ \hfill (E4)

If $V_1^{(2)}$ is the (8,4,3) code (as is the case for the GH-ARQ scheme based on (12,4,5) KM code), $\ell' = 4$ and $t_2 = 1$.

For system B, $E[A]$ is underbounded by,

$$E[A]_B < (P_c(1+2a_1) + a_2(2+a_1) + 3a_3) \cdot \frac{1}{(1-a_1)^2} \tag{E5}$$

where $a_1 = (1-P_c)^2 (1-P_t)$

$\qquad a_2 = (1-P_c) P_c$

and $\quad a_3 = (1-P_c)^2 P_t$

The probabilities q_0 and y are evaluated as follows,

$$q_0 = [\sum_{j=0}^{t_1} \binom{3\ell'}{j} \varepsilon^j (1-\varepsilon)^{3\ell'-j}]^{n/\ell'} \tag{E6}$$

$$y = (1-\varepsilon)^n [3\{\sum_{j=0}^{t_1} \binom{2\ell'}{j} \varepsilon^j (1-\varepsilon)^{2\ell'-j}\}^{n/\ell'}$$

$$- 3(1-\varepsilon)^n \{\sum_{j=0}^{t_1} \binom{\ell'}{j} \varepsilon^j (1-\varepsilon)^{\ell'-j}\}^{n/\ell'} \tag{E7}$$

$$- 5 (1-\varepsilon)^{2n}]$$

The expression for q_1 is same as (E4). If V_1 is the (12,4,5) code, $\ell'=4$ and $t_1 = 2$.

APPENDIX F

Reliability of GH-ARQ Schemes

It has been established that the type-II hybrid ARQ system provides the same order of system reliability as an ARQ system [32]. Similar arguments can also be used to establish that the GH-ARQ system provides the same order of reliability as an ARQ system.

Let E denote the event that the receiver of the GH-ARQ system accepts a block containing undetectable errors. The reliability of the GH-ARQ system can, therefore, be characterised by the probability of the event E, i.e. $Pr(E)$. Such a probability is given by,

$$Pr(E) = Pr(A_0^e) + \sum_{i=1}^{\infty} Pr(A_0^d \ E_1^d \ \ldots \ E_{i-1}^d \ E_i^e) \qquad (F1)$$

It has been stated earlier that the probabilities of the joint events required to evaluate the above expression are different to compute. In the following, we proceed to upperbound each of the terms in (F1).

In the GH-ARQ scheme of depth m, error-detection is performed on the basis of the codes having $\tilde{H}_i$, i=1,2,...,m as the parity check matrix. If P_{e_i} is the probability of undetected error for such codes, let $P_e = \max(P_{e_i}, i=1,2,...,m)$ and $P_f = \min (P_{e_i}, i=1,2,...,m)$.

Therefore,

$$Pr(A_0^e) \ \leqslant \ P_e$$

and

$$Pr(B_i^e) \ \leqslant \ P_e, \quad i = 1,2,\ldots$$

Also, the probability that errors are detected in any transmision is upperbounded by $1-P_c-P_f$. Let $P_d = 1-P_c-P_f$. Consider the term $Pr(A_0^d \ldots E_{i-1}^d \ E_{i-1}^d \ E_i^e)$. Since $E_i^d = B_i^d \ Q_i^d$ and $E_i^e = B_i^e \cup B_i^d \ Q_i^e$, we have

$$Pr(A_0^d \ldots E_{i-1}^d \ E_i^e) \ < \ Pr(A_0^d \ B_1^d \ldots B_{i-1}^d \ E_i^e)$$

$$= \ Pr(A_0^d \ B_1^d \ldots B_{i-1}^d) Pr(E_i^e | A_0^d \ldots B_{i-1}^d)$$

$$< \ P_d^i \ Pr(B_i^e \cup B_i^d \ Q_i^e | A_0^d \ldots B_{i-1}^d)$$

$$= \ P_d^i [\ Pr(B_i^e) + Pr(B_i^d) Pr(Q_i^e | A_0^d \ldots B_i^d)]$$

$$< \ P_d^i [P_e + P_d \ Pr(Q_i^e | A_0^d \ldots B_i^d)] \qquad (F2)$$

Since the decoded data block is checked for presence of errors at every retransmission, we have

$$Pr(Q_i^e | A_0^d \ldots B_i^d) \ < \ P_e \qquad (F3)$$

Substituting (F3) into (F2), we get,

$$Pr(A_0^d \ldots E_{i-1}^d \ E_i^e) \ < \ P_d^i \ (1 + P_d) \ P_e$$

Using the above expression, $Pr(E)$ can be upperbounded as,

$$Pr(E) \ < \ P_e + \sum_{i=1}^{\infty} P_d^i \ (1 + P_d) \ P_e$$

$$= \ (1 + P_d^2) \ \frac{P_e}{P_c + P_f}$$

$$= \ (1 + P_d^2) \ (1 + \frac{P_e - P_f}{P_c + P_f}) \ \frac{P_e}{P_c + P_e} \qquad (F4)$$

For a GH-ARQ system $P_d < 1$ and $P_c \gg P_e$; therefore,

$$1 + P_d^2 \ < \ 2$$

and $1 + \dfrac{P_e - P_f}{P_c + P_f} \approx 1.$ (F5)

Uisng (F5), the expression for Pr(E) is simplified to,

$$Pr(E) \leqslant 2 \cdot \dfrac{P_e}{P_c + P_e}$$ (F6)

For a pure ARQ system, using a code V_0 for error-detection having probability of undetected error P_e, the probability of the event E is given by [8],

$$Pr(E)_{ARQ} = \dfrac{P_e}{P_c + P_e}$$

and, therefore, $Pr(E) \leqslant 2Pr(E)_{ARQ}$.

It is clear from above that the GH-ARQ scheme provides the same order of reliability as a pure ARQ scheme using a code V_0 for error-detection having P_e as the probability of undetected error.

Lecture Notes in Control and Information Sciences

Edited by M. Thoma

Lecture Notes in Control and Information Sciences

Edited by M. Thoma and A. Wyner

Vol. 62: Analysis and Optimization
of Systems
Proceedings of the Sixth International
Conference on Analysis and Optimization
of Systems
Nice, June 19–22, 1984
Edited by A. Bensoussan, J. L. Lions
XIX, 591 pages. 1984.

Vol. 63: Analysis and O~~~~~~~~
of Systems
Proceedings of the (
Conference on Ana
of Systems
Nice, June 19–22, 1!
Edited by A. Bensou
XIX, 700 pages. 198

Vol. 64: Arunabha E
Stackelberg Differe
in Economic Model
VIII, 203 pages, 198

Vol. 65: Yaakov Yavi
Numerical Studies
in Nonlinear Filterin
VIII, 273 pages, 198

Vol. 66: Systems an
Proceedings of the
Enschede, The Net
Edited by A. Bagchi
X, 206 pages, 1985

Vol. 67: Real Time (
Proceedings of the
University of Patras
Edited by G. Schmi
S. Tzafestas
XI, 650 pages, 198

Vol. 68: T. Kaczorek
Two-Dimensional L
IX, 397 pages, 198

Vol. 69: Stochastic
Filtering and Contr
Proceedings of the
Marseille-Luminy, F
Edited by M. Metivi
X, 310 pages, 1985

Vol. 70: Uncertainty
Proceedings of a D
Bonn, Germany, M
Edited by J. Ackerm
IV, 236 pages, 198.

Vol. 71: N. Baba
New Topics in Learning Automata
Theory and Applications
VII, 231 pages, 1985.

Vol. 72: A. Isidori
Nonlinear Control Systems:
An Introduction
VI, 297 pages, 1985.

ler

d on
iques

r

national
984
ch,

ning
llo,

Honnef

elmes,

s

IV, 211 pages, 1986.